Establishing Ministry Training

A Manual for Programme Developers

Robert W. Ferris
Editor

William Carey Library
Pasadena, California, USA

Technical Editor: Susan Peterson
Cover Design: Jeff Northway

© 1995
World Evangelical Fellowship
Missions Commission

Published by:
William Carey Library
P.O. Box 40129
Pasadena, CA 91114
USA
Telephone: (818) 798-0819

ISBN 0-87808-262-X

Printed in the United States of America

Contents

APPENDICES

Preface

"Establishing," in the title of this manual, enfolds an intentional ambiguity. Often establishing speaks of originating, beginning, starting from nothing. As expressed in the first chapter, this book was conceived as a manual for those starting missionary training programmes, primarily in the Two-Thirds World. The World Evangelical Fellowship is heavily invested in promoting missionary vision and outreach worldwide through its Missions Commission, which sponsored this project. It is the prayer of every individual who contributed to this manual that the good news of Jesus Christ will speed to the ends of the earth as members of the worldwide church are equipped for ministries of cross-cultural disciple-making, church planting, and teaching (cf. Mt 28:19-20).

Sometimes, however, "establishing" refers to strengthening, making stable or firm something which exists. Around the world today, churches have started programmes or centres for missionary training. Many of these, however, are weak and struggling. Where financial resources are present, experienced personnel often are lacking and vice versa. Even where personnel and material resources are available, skills of curriculum planning and programme development often have been in short supply. Often missionary trainers have resorted to adapting from their Bible school experiences or innovating on the basis of their experiences in ministry. There is a better way. A second burden of this manual is to place in the hands of trainers a resource they can use to strengthen their ministry training programmes. We offer guidance for focusing on the understandings, skills, and character qualities needed by trainees, and for providing training appropriate to the trainees' culture and sensitive to cultures in which they will serve.

The word "ministry" in the title also deserves comment. As noted, missionary training (especially in the Two-Thirds World) provided the impetus and primary focus for writing this book.

Nevertheless, with very minor adaptations, the principles and guidelines laid out in this manual are applicable to a broad spectrum of ministry training contexts. The methods recommended are grounded on biblically and educationally informed theory and practice. The authors pray that Bible schools, seminaries, and church-based programmes of ministry training around the world, as well as missionary training centres, will find this manual useful.

The Origins of This Manual

In July, 1991, as part of the WEF Missions Commission International Missionary Training Project, a consultation on missionary training was held for the Southern Cone countries of Latin America. A featured event was the creation of a chart of "competencies" which an ideal cross-cultural missionary from that region should possess in order to be effective.

The technique used to create the first missionary training profile was adapted from an approach used primarily by vocational educators (Sinnett 1976; Mitchell 1983; Norton 1985). The DACUM (Developing A CurriculUM) process emerged during the 1960s and '70s as a method for determining the competencies needed to perform effectively in a given occupation. Essentially, a small group of expert practitioners employs a consensus process to create a comprehensive descriptive chart (also referred to as a competencies profile or a DACUM chart). The approach requires identifying in precise terms what trainees need to know, what they need to be able to do, and what attitudes they need to manifest. A second part of the exercise involves setting measurable standards of competence for each item on the chart.

The profile developed by missionary trainers in the Southern Cone nations was received with interest by the missionary training community around the world. Similar studies were subsequently conducted in other WEF Missions Commission sponsored or independent consultations in Latin America, Africa, Asia, and the Caribbean. Participants in these consultations also produced other profiles in their own contexts. Attracted by the Latin American project, the Indian Missions Association invited the WEF Missions Commission to facilitate a similar profiling exercise as part of the Association's annual conference in September, 1992.

Reflection on WEF's experience with profiling projects to that point led to the conclusion that the process employed should be further developed. In addition to competencies (re-termed "ministry skills"), our study of the Bible alerted us to character qualifications for spiritual leadership which the original DACUM process did not address. We also recognise that an over-emphasis on ministry roles and competencies can mislead missionary trainers.

Missionary work, first and last, must be a work of God. The principal qualification for ministry, therefore, is not cross-cultural communication skills, effective evangelism technique, professionally implemented church planting strategies, or even strong relational and leadership skills. The principal qualification for missionary service—indeed, for all ministry—is an intimate knowledge of God; without a personal and daily experience of the awe and power of God, all of our professionalism is hollow. We must never permit curriculum planning to become a choice between godliness and professionalism; we need both. Curriculum planning which focuses excessively on roles and competencies can lead us to neglect the one indispensable source of power and authority in ministry.

Thus, we significantly altered the DACUM research approach in order to produce a more relevant profile of missionary qualifications. We remain convinced of the value of a goal oriented approach to curriculum planning and incorporate this component into a process which will allow missionary training planners to move beyond "competencies."

As the need for missionary training around the world exploded, two recognitions became clear. First, more comprehensive educational assistance is needed by new and struggling programmes. Profiling is a useful tool, but procedures for clarifying shared values, framing teaching goals, writing learning objectives, designing learning experiences, and evaluating learning outcomes also are needed. Second, it is both inappropriate and unrealistic for the evangelical missions community worldwide to be dependent for technical expertise on a handful of Western educators.

The WEF Missions Commission has responded to these recognitions in two ways. In February, 1994, the Missionary Training Consultants' Seminar was held in Pasadena, California. At that seminar, ninety-six missionary trainers from thirty-two nations received instruction and observed or participated in demonstrations of the principles in this book. The second response was commitment to publish the training given at that seminar; the manual you hold in your hand is the realisation of that goal.

We are greatly encouraged by the enthusiastic acceptance of the profiling exercise, the training offered at the Missionary Training Consultants' Seminar, and the ensuing consideration of outcome-based training. We believe the principles and methods in this manual can be of great help to trainers in establishing programmes which produce effective workers for the harvest.

A Word About Words

We have attempted to write in standard English. Where educational jargon is useful, we have included definitions or explanations. Educational books are full of debates over the use of words and the difference of meaning between purpose, goal, objective, outcome, etc. To avoid being distracted by debates over language, you may translate the concepts presented in this book into whatever terms you prefer.

Some Christian educators make a point of distinguishing between *teaching* (i.e., facilitating or helping people learn) and *training* (i.e., using behavioural techniques to cause people to acquire desired skills—as you "train" an animal to do tricks). Since the growing field of training serves human beings and their organisations in myriad ways, we reject this negative use of the term "training" and will use it synonymously with the term "teaching." Both teaching and training contribute directly and indirectly to the wellness and success of individuals and organisations—families, churches, missions, and businesses.

Introducing the Authors

This manual was a collaborative effort from the beginning. The general outline of the book was conceived by Jon Lewis, Steve Hoke, and Bob Ferris in sessions preparatory to the International Missionary Training Consultants' Seminar, mentioned above. As the manual has developed, we have continued to interact with one another; at this point it is quite impossible to isolate any one individual's contribution. Nevertheless, some reader may be interested in the diversity of backgrounds and experiences reflected in the pages which follow. The authors are introduced in the order of the chapters which they contributed.

Robert Ferris grew up in the home of a Baptist pastor who was deeply committed to world evangelisation. When Bob was eleven, his parents answered God's call to a church-planting ministry which was greatly blessed by God in Liberia's Sino County. A graduate of Wheaton College and Denver Seminary, Bob and his wife, Sue, served for twenty-one years with SEND International in the Republic of the Philippines. Bob and Sue went to the Philippines to teach theology and New Testament at Febias College of Bible, but after seven years Bob recognised his need for educational training. After completing a Ph.D. at Michigan State University, Bob and his family returned to the Philippines, where Bob provided educational services to Bible school and TEE educators through two interdenominational associations of ministry trainers. In 1984 Bob became dean of Asian Theological Seminary in Manila. Throughout the 1980s Bob also served with the International Council of Accrediting Agencies, a project of WEF's Theological Commission.

Bob is a consultant, speaker, and author on issues of theology and education in ministry training. He has several published articles, including six on accreditation of theological education. Bob also wrote *Renewal in Theological Education* while serving as the 1988-89 missionary scholar in residence at the Billy Graham Center in Wheaton, Illinois. Bob is the primary author of Chapters 1, 3, and 6, joint author of Chapter 2, and the general editor of this manual. Bob and Sue have two children, both of whom were born and graduated from high school in the Philippines, and one grandson.

Jonathan Lewis was born in Argentina, where his father was a missionary evangelist, pastor, and editor of a pre-evangelism periodical which developed a continent-wide circulation. Personally impressed with the importance of training ministries, Jon began his own missionary career in 1974 in Honduras, where he worked closely with Conservative Baptist missionary and TEE pioneer, George Patterson. Since then, Jon and his wife, Dawn, have served the Lord and his church in Mexico, Peru, and Argentina. Jon continued his own preparation, completing an M.A. in education at Portland State University and a Ph.D. in vocational education at Colorado State University. Currently, Jon and Dawn are busy launching a cross-cultural missionary training centre in Argentina's Cordoba Province at the request of the Argentine church. By God's grace, this centre will be the first of its kind in the Southern Cone nations of Spanish America.

Since 1993, Jon has served as Assistant Director for Latin America with the WEF Missions Commission. In that role he recently assumed the editorship of *Training for Cross-Cultural Ministry*, the Mission Commission's periodical newsletter. Jon also has edited *World Mission: An Analysis of the World Christian Movement* (a revision of the popular *Perspectives on the World Christian Movement*) and *Working Your Way to the Nations: A Guide to Effective Tentmaking*. In the present manual, Jon is the primary author of Chapter 2. Jon and Dawn have four children, two boys and two girls; the oldest is seventeen and the youngest is seven.

Stephen Hoke traveled to Japan at the age of two with his missionary parents and spent the next fifteen years in that nation. Steve's father served as church planter and missionary educator with TEAM, planting three churches while helping to launch Tokyo Christian University and Japan Bible Seminary. Growing up in Japan provided a strong background for Steve's continuing investment in cross-cultural ministry and missionary training. After completing bachelor's and master's degrees at Wheaton College, Steve served on the staff of the 1974 Lausanne Congress on Evangelism. He completed an M.Div. at Trinity Evangelical Divinity School and a Ph.D. in nonformal adult education from Michigan State University. He has taught missions at Seattle Pacific University, was Associate Director of Field Training for World Vision, and most recently served as President of LIFE Ministries (Japan). Currently, Steve is Vice President of Staff Training and Development with Church Resource Ministries (CRM), based in southern California. With CRM, he helps prepare U.S. and international teams for ministry, encourages and mentors staff in their personal development, and coaches staff in developing training materials. He also works outside of CRM with other North America-based and Two-Thirds World mission agencies as a training specialist.

Steve has helped train over 1,000 people for cross-cultural ministry and has authored numerous popular articles on missions. In this manual, he is the primary author of Chapters 4 and 5. Steve and his wife, Eloise, have two teenage children, Stephenie and Christopher.

Lois Fuller is a Canadian missionary with World Partners of the Missionary Church/EMC of Canada, who has lived and worked in Nigeria for the past twenty-one years. The commitment of Lois's parents to world missions bore fruit in the lives of three of their six children—Lois and two missionary brothers, one serving with Lois in Nigeria and the other with FEBA in the Seychelles. Lois's preparation for ministry included studies at Emmanuel Bible College, the University of Guelph (linguistics), and Trinity Evangelical Divinity School (New Testament). Lois's ministry in Nigeria has been invested in ministry training. For fourteen years she taught Greek and Bible at United Missionary Theological College (UMTC), and she served for six years as dean of Nigeria Evangelical Missionary Institute (NEMI). Currently, Lois is helping to launch a missionary training programme at UMTC.

While at NEMI, Lois authored four books: *Going to the Nations: An Introduction to Cross-Cultural Missions, The Missionary and His Work, A Missionary Handbook on African Traditional Religion,* and *Adventurers for God: Stories of Missionary Pioneers.* She also co-edited *A Nation to Win: Nigeria National Survey.* In the present manual, Lois is the primary author of Chapter 7 and joint author of Chapter 3. Lois enjoys reading and camping.

Rodolfo Girón is an architect, a graduate of San Carlos University in his native Guatemala. Called by God to a ministry of pastoral leadership, evangelism, and missions, Rudy has been active in ministry since 1978. An ordained minister of the Church of God, Rudy completed his M.Div. in Cleveland, Tennessee. Since returning to Guatemala in 1984, he has pastored for five years and served as National Director of Theological Education for the Church of God in Guatemala, overseeing both residential and TEE programmes. In 1985 Rudy became involved with the emerging missions movement in Latin America through COMIBAM '87. Since 1990 he has served as President of COMIBAM, promoting and facilitating missions throughout Latin America.

Currently, while leading COMIBAM and expanding his ministry through the WEF Missions Commission, Rudy also is pursuing Doctor of Ministry studies. His contribution to this manual, Chapter 8, is unique in that the material was not conceived as a major presentation for the 1994 Missionary Training Consultants' Seminar. Rather, it was presented as a morning devotional message. The power and pertinence of Rudy's application of biblical truth to the task of programme development—specifically, his warning of dangers inherent in cross-cultural application of Western educational technology—demands our attention. Rudy and his wife, Alma, have four teenage children. When he is not traveling or ministering, Rudy enjoys spending time with his family, reading good literature, making music, and visiting with friends.

Acknowledgements

We would be remiss to close this preface without acknowledging the assistance of others. Dr. William D. Taylor, WEF Missions Commission Director, has been a source of support and encouragement to all of us. It is at his initiative and through the resources of the Missions Commission that the Missionary Training Consultants' Seminar was held and that this manual is published. Together, the authors express their gratitude to Bill.

Appreciation also is due to Columbia Biblical Seminary (CBS) for awarding Bob Ferris a faculty study leave during fall semester, 1994, to edit this manual. Dr. Kenneth Mulholland, CBS Dean, and Dr. Johnny Miller, President of Columbia International University, are specifically to be thanked.

We acknowledge the contribution of colleagues from all nations with whom we have worked and from whom we have learned. The participants in the 1994 Missionary Training Consultants' Seminar stimulated us and helped us clarify our thoughts and expressions. Special thanks is due to our families. Lois's chapter was written in Nigeria but was rewritten at her sister's home in Belleville, Ontario. The rest of us have worked on our writing among other responsibilities, often at the expense of sleep or family time. We praise God for those who love us and who share our passion to equip workers for the harvest.

Finally, we praise God for his grace in our lives. We pray that this manual will contribute toward his goal of filling heaven with worshippers from every nation, every tribe, every people, and every language.

Robert Ferris, Editor

World Evangelical Fellowship Missions Commission

World Evangelical Fellowship and its member organisations exist to establish and help regional and national evangelical alliances empower and mobilise local churches and Christian organisations to disciple the nations for Christ.

WEF Missions Commission is a global network of national missions leaders, with many of its members fulfilling wider international roles with their own ministries.

Our overarching purpose is to equip the church and, in particular, the regional and national missions alliances to carry out the Great Commission.

Our vision is to serve as an international partnering-networking team that shares ideas, information and resources to empower the global missions movement to effectively train and send missionaries. We do this by affirming and facilitating the vision of regional and national missions leaders.

A Word of History

From WEF's inception, a global passion has motivated its leadership. The emergence of active, indigenous missionary movements in Asia, Africa, Latin America, the South Pacific, the Caribbean and the Middle East was the primary catalyst that led to the official launching of the Missions Commission (MC) in 1977. The MC's fundamental intention was to address worldwide missions issues of common concern to its member bodies, with particular interest for these newly emerged and now maturing non-Western missionary movements. The MC also serves as the primary global evangelical missionary alliance, linking the continents in a spirit of inter-dependent partnership.

Objectives

1. To promote dynamic cooperation among existing and emerging national and regional missions associations by providing a platform for:

- expressing relational and informational networking
- establishing national missions commissions
- forging strategic alliances and partnerships

2. To strengthen and aid in the development of sending churches, training programmes, and support/shepherding structures by:

- facilitating the use of experienced consultant resources
- publishing and distributing vital information and didactic materials
- facilitating the training of key Two-Thirds World missions leaders

3. To address critical concerns of international evangelical missions structures and their national and regional associations to achieve defined ends by:

- convening strategic international conferences and consultations
- creating investigative task forces to address critical needs within global missions
- administering projects and programmes

OPERATIONAL UNITS

The Missions Commission carries out its objectives through the following five operational units:

1. Membership Network

The MC membership currently includes two primary categories: *general members* and *consultants*. This participatory body is kept informed of MC activities and represents it before constituencies in their own part of the world. Members and consultants are nominated by the WEF Executive Committee and approved by the WEF International Council.

The Missions Commission reiterates one of its original values: to help establish national missionary associations where they do not exist, and to strengthen those which ask for help. By so doing we also help fulfill the overarching mission statement of WEF.

General Membership: The MC draws its membership primarily from WEF member associations. Executive officers of regional missions associations are automatically invited to be part of the MC. Other leaders from national missions agencies or associations may be invited to serve on the basis of their specific gifting and contribution to the work of the MC. The normal term of service in WEF commissions is four years, subject to review at two-year periods. The complete list of our membership is available upon request.

Consultants: In addition to the general membership, the MC Executive Committee may invite into membership persons who are specialists in missions by virtue of their experience and training, but who do not qualify for regular membership because they are not directly involved in a member association. The normal term of service is two years.

The MC is led by the Executive Committee (ExCo), which is comprised of one invited representative from each of the continental missions associations, whose nomination must be approved by the WEF International Council (IC). The ExCo with the approval of the WEF/IC appoints a Commission Director. The ExCo also supervises his work, approves staff appointments, reviews and approves the annual ministry goals and budget, and seeks the general welfare of the MC. Other members of the ExCo include the Director and invited staff members. The current MC staff include Dr. William Taylor (USA) and Dr. Jonathan Lewis (Argentina) on a full-time basis. Dr. Raymond Windsor (New Zealand) and Arq. Rudy Girón (Guatemala) serve on a half-time basis.

2. International Missionary Training Programme (IMTP)

Missionary training represents the MC's major resource commitment since 1988. As training programmes have emerged and matured, the MC has modified its programmes in light of new opportunities and changing needs.

This long-term project was initiated in 1989 during the Manila Consultation on Missionary Training, where sixty leaders from around the world discussed critical issues in missionary training. The papers presented at this strategic conference were later published under the title *Internationalising Missionary Training: A Global Perspective*, ed. William D. Taylor (Paternoster, 1991).

This consultation led to the initiation of the IMTP, the International Missionary Training Fellowship (IMTF), the International Missionary Trainers Scholarship Programme (IMTS), and eventually, the International Missionary Training Associates (IMTA) programmes. The IMTP became an on-going programme of the WEF/MC in 1993.

International Missionary Training Fellowship (IMTF)

Through on-going research, this programme seeks to identify missionary training programmes around the world and links them together through a directory published every three years and distributed to each member. Dr. Windsor served as the first editor of *Training for Cross-Cultural Ministries*, a post held now by Dr. Lewis. This unique publication focuses on training issues and gives news and information appropriate to the global missionary leadership as well as the training community. It is sent to over 1,000 leaders and over 500 training centres around the world.

International Missionary Training Associates (IMTA)

Missionary training resource persons are being steadily recruited, trained, and mobilised to help achieve the ends of the MC. Currently twelve additional leaders form the IMTA team and actively serve in consultant roles. MC staff members are all considered IMTAs.

International Missionary Trainers Scholarship Programme (IMTS)

This programme is designed to empower, through advanced missiological studies, key men and women with clear potential contribution to missions and missionary training in their own national context. They are encouraged to apply to the MC for scholarship funding.

3. WEF/MC Publications Programme

Based on established needs, the WEF/MC contracts the production of key books and texts, and it helps publish and distribute these and other titles which meet critical missions needs in different parts of the world. When necessary, appropriate translation and adaptation are carried out. Dr. Lewis serves as the publications coordinator.

4. International Missionary Research Project (IMRP)

This task force represents a major departure from previous projects and programmes in its focus, reach, and breadth. If the unevangelised and under-evangelised peoples and cities of the world are to be effectively "reached" and strong churches established, Christians worldwide must send out and sustain on the field a well-equipped, long-term, global, cross-cultural missionary force. Both the Western and non-Western missionary movement experience a disturbing career missionary attrition rate. The problems approach crisis status in some non-Western missions, and no study has ever attempted to identify and address their attrition issues.

The broader goal of the study is to increase the overall efficiency and effectiveness of the global missionary force in completing the Great Commission by reducing the undesirable attrition rate of career missionaries.

The specific research objective is to identify and verify the causes for undesirable attrition by Western and non-Western missionaries and then suggest the ways and means of dealing constructively with them.

With these points in mind, we have three strategic context dimensions as they relate to the research issues:

- the pre-candidate context
- the training context
- the field context

5. Task Force on Tentmaking

This task force relates to other evangelical world bodies in the discussion and promotion of tentmaking missionaries. WEF/MC has cooperated with the Lausanne Tentmakers International Exchange (TIE) to participate in effective global networking. The MC revitalised its Tentmaking Task Force in July 1994, during a Singapore meeting. Coordinated by Mr. Loh Hoe Peng of Singapore, the Task Force has articulated its objectives in light of the WEF mission statement:

1. To encourage the church to develop its potential as a tentmaking seedbed.

2. To facilitate tentmakers worldwide.

3. To provide an enabling link between agencies and the church in tentmaking.

4. To provide additional instructional resources.

5. To develop a global directory of tentmaking networks.

This task force, under the editorship of Dr. Jonathan Lewis, produced a strategic twelve-chapter course in workbook form, *Working Your Way to the Nations: A Guide to Effective Tentmaking.* This workbook utilises twelve authors from ten different countries, for adaptation and publication in six languages.

If the WEF Missions Commission can be of service to you, please do not hesitate to contact us at one of our international offices.

William D. Taylor, Director
WEF Missions Commission
4807 Palisade Drive
Austin, TX 78731
USA
Tel: 512 467 8431 / Fax: 512 467 2849

World Evangelical Fellowship
International Headquarters
141 Middle Road, #05-05
GSM Building
SINGAPORE 0718
Tel: 65 339 7900 / Fax: 65 338 3756

World Evangelical Fellowship
North American Offices
P.O. Box WEF
Wheaton, IL 60189
USA
Tel: 708 668 0440 / Fax: 708 669 0498

Chapter 1

Building Consensus on Training Commitments

Robert Ferris

The church of Jesus Christ is growing faster today than at any time since our Lord gave his Great Commission. More men, women, and children have entered God's kingdom and more churches have been planted in the past decade than in any similar period in history. Centuries of prayer for the nations and years of missiological focus on church planting and church growth are bearing fruit in our generation. Despite evidences of decline in vital Christianity in the West and continued resistance to the gospel among some people groups, God's worldwide church is growing.

Just as encouraging as the numerical growth of the church, however, is the growth of missionary vision within churches which, until recently, were recipients of missionary outreach. Around the globe, the younger churches have caught the vision of world evangelisation and are joining the missionary force in mind-boggling numbers. More than 4,000 cross-cultural missionaries have been commissioned by Indian churches, primarily in South and Northeast India. The Korean church reports 3,272 missionaries serving with 113 agencies in 119 nations in 1994 (Moon 1994:8). From Nigeria, Kenya, the Philippines, Singapore, Brazil, Argentina, and scores of other nations around the globe come additional reports of growth in the missionary task force. It is projected that, by the end of this century—which is nearly upon us!—the number of Christian missionaries from the Two-Thirds World will outnumber those from Western Europe and North America (Pate 1991:35).

This explosion of Two-Thirds World missions holds, at once, the greatest promise and the greatest challenge for world evangelisation. The promise is clear; the challenge is that this task force must be equipped for cross-cultural ministry. Skills required for life in an alien culture are not intuitive. Cross-cultural communication is more complex than learning a new language. Relational models and metaphors appropriate in one's home culture may translate very differently into a new setting. Many Two-Thirds World churches have learned by sad experience a lesson Western missions learned decades ago: The work of world evangelisation can be hastened and the rate of missionary "casualties" slowed by first training missionary volunteers.

This does not imply that Western models of missionary training should be replicated throughout the Two-Thirds World. Monolingual, monocultural Koreans may face some of the same challenges as monolingual, monocultural Americans, but differences between Korean and American cultures represent unique areas of challenge as well. Multilingual, multicultural Indians or Filipinos may come better prepared to handle some challenges, but they may need preparation in other areas.

Consider, as well, the nature of missionary training in the West. With few exceptions, candidates are advised to enroll in a Bible school or seminary in preparation for career missionary service. Most mission organisations run "orientation" programmes for new missionaries, lasting from a few days to a few weeks, but the principal task of missionary preparation is delegated to the Bible school or seminary. This model assumes the wealth required to support Western schooling institutions and the capacity of missionary volunteers to disengage from work and family responsibilities for the years needed to pursue a degree. These conditions rarely occur among Two-Thirds World churches.

The response of churches in many parts of the world has been to develop centres dedicated to preparing missionaries for cross-cultural ministry.[1] Typically these centres operate with a small

---

1. See the recently published *World Directory of Missionary Training Programs* for a list of 514 centres worldwide. It should be noted, however, that most of the North American centres included in this directory are, in fact, Bible schools or seminaries and therefore do not fit the description of a missionary training centre provided here.

staff of missionaries or former missionaries, who offer a highly focused curriculum of centre-based and field-based learning experiences, often with meager facilities and financial support.[2] Missionary training centre programmes vary enormously, reflecting the diverse needs of missionary trainees, but also the differing resources and skills of missionary trainers. Despite the high motivations and sacrificial service of training staff, it must be acknowledged that there also is wide variance in the effectiveness of training offered by these centres.

All missionary trainers want to train effectively. Whether the centre is a new one which is just beginning or an established centre with an operating programme, the key to developing effective missionary training is a person we shall term "the programme developer." The programme developer must have a vision for effective missionary training in his or her own context. The programme developer also must have the authority to exercise initiative toward launching or modifying the missionary training programme. This authority may come from appointment by a church, a mission agency, or an association of mission agencies, or it may come from the programme developer's recognised capacity to rally churches and mission agencies to the cause of missionary training. It is not essential for the programme developer to be an experienced, long-term, cross-cultural missionary, but prior, successful missionary service is a great advantage.

The task of the programme developer is to conceive and implement strategies for missionary training in the new or existing missionary training centre. Fortunately, this is not—and must not become—a one-person task. The programme developer should function much like an orchestra conductor, coordinating programme development activities, calling on different groups or individuals when their contribution is especially needed, and providing the unifying vision and leadership for the overall task.

---

2. For a very helpful and much fuller description of missionary training centres, see C. David Harley, *Preparing to Serve: Training for Cross-Cultural Mission*. Dr. Harley's helpful book reflects the experience of some of the most developed missionary training centres and provides wise and informed advice on the design and operation of a missionary training centre. As such, it is a companion volume to this book.

The approach to programme development presented in this book recognises the contribution of three distinct groups within the missionary training community. The experience and insight of missionaries and mission leaders is especially critical in developing a profile of an effective missionary.[3] Missionary educators—especially personnel directors of mission agencies, deans of Bible schools, and the missionary training centre director—must co-ordinate the over-all task of missionary preparation.[4] The task of developing a specific programme of training and of organising the experiences which implement the programme ultimately must rest with the training unit staff.[5]

Assumptions Are Unavoidable

Everything we do, every choice we make is preceded by other factors. This is true of our daily lives, and it is true of missionary training programme development as well. Indeed, our actions and choices reflect assumptions about what is real, about what is true, and about what is important.[6] The problem is this: Although we all make decisions based on assumptions, often those assumptions are unexamined. We even may be unaware of the assumptions which shape our lives and which underlie our training programmes.

Indeed, the problem is more serious still. Just as everything we do and choose is based on assumptions, the same is true of others as well. When I read about a training method and decide I want to incorporate it into my training programme, I must be aware that this method has grown out of *someone's* assumptions about the real, the true, and the important. The method is appropriate, given their assumptions. But does it fit my assumptions? And how can

---

3. The procedure for developing a missionary profile is explained in Chapter 2 of this book.

4. Chapter 3 outlines responsibilities shared by missionary educators.

5. Chapters 4, 5, and 6 are designed to guide and assist programme staff.

6. In the language of philosophy, these areas are referred to as ontology, epistemology, and axiology. The three make up the major divisions of classical philosophy.

I be sure, if their assumptions are unstated and if my own assumptions are unexamined?

A second factor which shapes our actions and decisions—and, thus, our training programmes—is our values, the preferences and priorities which direct our lives. Values are different from assumptions, in that they are specifically chosen. Usually it is easier for us to express our values than to express our assumptions. A great deal of attention within the social sciences has been given to values in recent years. An underlying assumption in most of the resulting literature, however, is that values are morally neutral, shaped by culture and personal experience. Because naturalistic social scientists assume values are relative, they also believe it is no more appropriate to question a person's values than to question their tastes in food, clothing, or music.

Evangelical Christians, however, cannot be comfortable with unexamined assumptions or with unquestionable values. This is because the Bible claims to be the very Word of God and because it provides clear and consistent teaching about the kind of person God is, about the kind of world he created, and about how he intends men and women to live. The Bible provides a standard for judging our assumptions and values.

As a matter of fact, when God instructed his people how to recognise error in their midst, he mandated two tests: (1) whatever is true will be consistent with prior truth, i.e., with God's revelation, now recorded in the Bible (Dt 13:1-5) and (2) whatever is true will be consistent with evidence from the world God created (Dt 18:21-22). The New Testament also admonishes Christians to apply the tests of consistency (Gal 1:6-9; 1 Jn 4:1-3).

The assumptions and values which underlie our actions and decisions, as well as those of others who influence us, must be exposed and tested, biblically and evidentially. Any assumption or value which is inconsistent with God's Word or which is contradicted by the reality of the world God created must be abandoned. On the other hand, we can build our lives—and our missionary training programmes—with confidence on those assumptions and values which are consistent with and affirmed by the Bible and empirical evidence.

Because assumptions often are unexamined and values are unquestioned, we need a different term to designate the tested foundations on which our training programmes will be built. In the pages which follow, we will refer to tested assumptions and values as "commitments." Besides connoting testing, "commitment" also focuses on a willing decision to accept and act on the truth or value represented.

Commitments Shape Training Programmes

As we consider programmes for missionary training, there are at least six areas in which assumptions need to be examined and commitments established. While this should not be considered an exhaustive list, it will prove a fruitful beginning point for thinking and discussion. With each area, we have identified biblical or empirical (i.e., social science) evidence which appears relevant.

1. The **specific goals** of missionary training—the ends which guide training decisions and, even more important, how those ends are identified.

Traditionally, educators have looked to two sources when faced with decisions regarding the material and structure of training. Most commonly, perhaps, they consult the experience of others. "What are other schools doing?" is a question which surfaces, sooner or later, in almost every curriculum discussion. "How has this been handled historically?" and "What is a good textbook on this subject?" are alternative versions of the same question. These questions are not inappropriate; only a fool insists on making all mistakes himself! We can learn much from the insights and experience of others, and we must be willing to do so. Whatever other evidence we consider, this certainly has a place. Nevertheless, learning from others may not be as straight-forward as it appears. The example of others is most useful when training goals and contexts are identical. In missionary training—especially when viewed cross-culturally—that almost never is the case. A measure of caution, therefore, is needed.

A second basis for training decisions is a rational analysis of the discipline field or the content to be taught. This strategy holds enormous benefit for the trainer as well as the trainee. In the process of analysis, the trainer often obtains insights which promote mastery of the subject matter and facilitate instruction of learners. Whereas the experience of others affords a broadened perspective for making training decisions, rational analysis provides confidence in decision-making, since the trainer has made the subject field his or her own.

Scripture also provides guidance for those making training decisions. God intends his people to be Christlike and fruitful (Eph 4:13-16; Jn 15:5). The New Testament also identifies specific qualities and abilities which should characterise believers and leaders in Christ's church (1 Tim 3:1-7; 2 Tim 2:24-26; Tit 1:6-10). We also find that the Holy Spirit gives spiritual "gifts" or abilities to all believers (1 Cor 12:4-11), yet the Spirit's giving of these gifts does not preclude the need of believers to be "equipped" to use their gifts effectively (Eph 4:11-12). This "equipping" ministry, in fact, affords perspective on the task of the missionary trainer.

Since we honour God when we do our work well, it seems clear that missionary training should be intentional and purposeful. The purposefulness of our training acquires focus when we first identify those qualities and capacities needed for spiritual maturity and effective ministry. While the wisdom of other trainers and our own rational analysis of the training task provide a context for decision-making, we can proceed with greater confidence if training decisions are grounded on the experience and insight of effective missionaries and mission leaders.

In this manual we provide instructions for conducting a "profiling" exercise which collects this information. We also show you how to transform a ministry profile into specific training goals. We encourage you to consider carefully this approach to identifying specific goals which can guide decisions that shape your missionary training programme or which can furnish criteria to assess the training your programme provides.

2.   The **context** of missionary training—the setting in which
     it is provided.

Missionary training in North America and Western Europe often is very individualistic, and it usually occurs in schools. An individual Christian may conclude from reading the Bible or from a heart stirred by missionary challenge that God is calling him or her to missionary service. The missionary volunteer then assumes responsibility for attending a Christian school for training and finally seeks God's guidance to a mission agency and a field of service.

When this pattern is imported into non-Western churches, it often creates many problems. Few societies outside North America and Western Europe are as individualistic as this model assumes. Furthermore, schooling is a very expensive way to obtain training, since it requires support of an administrative staff and faculty and usually a campus as well. To justify such expense, schools usually train more generally, with emphasis on information and theory (areas they handle well) and with less attention to training for specific ministries. Often the skills which are omitted are those most critical to cross-cultural effectiveness.

When we look to the Scriptures for guidance, we find a society which was much more community oriented. God deals with people as families and communities (Gen 12:1-4; Ex 19:3-8; 1 Pt 2:4-5, 9-10). Corporate life also was central to the early church (Ac 2:41-47; cf. the many uses of the phrase "one another" in the New Testament).

Educational research also informs us that a nurturing community can facilitate significant learning. Interaction promotes reflective learning. Social support and reinforcement encourage learning and its application in life.

When considering the appropriate context of training, trainers will want to think about the role of the church. How can the trainee's home congregation or other congregations in the area become partners in and context for missionary training? What other natural communities can be accessed to promote and expedite the training task? How can we create a learning community within the training centre? Corporate reflection on such questions can lead to culturally appropriate alternatives to Western patterns of individualism and schooling.

3. *The **structure** of missionary training—its relational and institutional context.*

Missionary training occurs both by and for leadership. The purpose of missionary training is to equip individuals who can lead the church in mission. Yet training itself entails leadership. This alerts us to the critical nature of the example we provide. The way we relate to trainees and the ways those relationships are institutionalised in our training programmes will directly impact trainees' understanding and exercise of leadership in ministry.

Jesus taught leadership by metaphor and example. The metaphor of the steward (or trustee—Lk 16:10-12) emphasises the accountability of a leader. Jesus' most developed leadership metaphor was the shepherd (Jn 10:1-15; 21:15-17; cf. 1 Pt 5:2-4), emphasising the intimacy of relationship which the leader has for those under his or her care. Perhaps his most striking metaphor, however, was the servant (Mk 10:42-45; Jn 13:12-17), focusing on the self-giving spirit of biblical leadership. Jesus not only taught this quality of leadership, he modelled it. In the process, he also provided the ultimate example for us as leaders (Phil 2:5-8).

Secular models of leadership (even within the church!) seek and exercise authority and power. Biblical leadership, in contrast, is oriented to responsibility (for those led) and accountability (to God). Secular leaders ask, "How can I get these people to do what I want?" Biblical leaders ask, "How can I promote the welfare of these people for whom God has made me responsible?"

Because example is such an effective teacher, the relationships we model and the structures by which we implement those relationships must be appropriate to our training goals. Hierarchical structures and authoritarian behaviours are fundamentally counter-productive to the goal of developing biblical leaders. We—and our training programmes—must model what we teach. Transforming instruction demands transformed mentors and models; we cannot teach what we have not learned or lived.

4.   *The **learner** and strategies of missionary training—the "who" of training.*

Whom we seek to train influences the selection of training strategies in at least two significant ways. Decisions on training strategies must consider the learner's preferred ways of learning and the experiences the learner brings to the learning task.

An important and distinctive aspect of culture is worldview. Culturally conditioned language supplies the categories by which we order experience and influences the ways we think. Furthermore, social interaction reinforces shared ways of viewing life and experience.

Perceptual frames and cognitive styles differ from individual to individual (Bolton 1977). Some tend to view life holistically, whereas others deal with life issue by issue, case by case. Some approach problem solving relationally, while others think individualistically. Some naturally think analytically, dissecting experience to achieve understanding, while others naturally think synthetically, combining and relating experiences to attain a grander view. None of these contrasts (or several others which could be added) is inherently right or wrong, better or worse, but they are different. That differentness is significant for decisions regarding training strategies.

Since culture influences the way individuals construct their understandings, it is not surprising that particular cognitive styles predominate in any given society. Learning progresses most efficiently when account is taken of individual and cultural perspectives and processes. A trainer is wise to factor cognitive style into decisions on training strategies. This warns us that, even when two programmes share a common training goal, the preferred route to that goal may be different.

The second element affecting decisions on training strategies is the learner's experience (Knowles 1980; Brookfield 1986). Unlike children, adult trainees bring to learning a wealth of experience on which they can build. Inevitably, however, the relevance of prior experience to specific learning tasks may vary, and that variation is significant for decisions on training strategy. When an adult learner has little or no prior experience in a specific area, directive, didactic strategies are appropriate. As trainees acquire perspective and relevant experience, however, training strategies can be selected which are more participative, allowing learners to build on that experience. Thus, decisions regarding trainer roles and strategies should be responsive to trainee competence.

5.   The **types of learning** and strategies of missionary training—the "what" of training.

In addition to considering the learner, decisions on training strategies also must suit the learning task. It is helpful to consider four types of learning which commonly occur in ministry training—specifically, theory, information, skills, and character qualities.[7]

Theory, whether theological, social, or educational, seeks to describe reality. As such, theory makes truth claims which need to be tested. Throughout history, philosophers have proposed various theories regarding the nature and appropriate tests of truth.

While the Scriptures do not address this subject directly, there are two passages in Deuteronomy which appear relevant. In both cases, Israel posed the question, "How can we recognise a false prophet?" Thus, the issue really was one of testing truth claims. In the first passage (Dt 13:1-3), the test given is one of logical consistency with prior revelation; if the prophet's message contradicts prior revelation, it is false and to be rejected. The second passage (Dt 18:21-22) provides a complementary test. In this case the message is to be examined for consistency with events in the observable world; if the prophet's message "does not take place or come true"—i.e., if it is inconsistent with observable evidence—it

---

7. Bloom (1956) divided learning into three domains: cognitive, psycho- motor, and affective. We have chosen to divide Bloom's cognitive domain into theory and information, recognising differences in the ways these areas are taught and tested. We also prefer the less technical term "skills" for Bloom's "psycho-motor domain" and have abandoned his "affective" category. It is our contention that character qualities are much more substantial than "affects" (i.e., feelings).

This, by the way, is an excellent illustration of how assumptions shape theory and language. Bloom, as a naturalistic behaviourist, does not recognise the reality of anything beyond the physical and electrochemical interactions in our bodies. Christians, who reject Bloom's assumptions, must reinterpret his findings in categories consistent with a biblical understanding of life and learning.

is to be rejected as false. In both cases the test is consistency, the one logical, the other evidential.

The same tests will serve us well in testing—and teaching—theory. Theories should be examined for logical consistency—internal, as well as with biblical revelation—and for factual consistency with all available evidence. Theories taught to trainees should be verified biblically, logically, and evidentially. In doing so, we also should be explicit about our methods, equipping trainees to test the truth claims of other theories they encounter.

Information makes up the majority content of most ministry training programmes. It often is said that we live in an "information age," that information is "exploding." Together with theory, information is the principal currency of schooling. Common strategies for acquiring information include reading, listening (e.g., to a lecture), memorising, and observing.

It is interesting to note that the biblical writers view "knowing" in a way quite unfamiliar to those raised in the Western schooling tradition. While the Hebrew verb "to know" (*YADA*) is used "to know by observing and reflecting," it also has the sense of "to know by experiencing" (Unger and White 1980:212; cf. Botterweck 1986). It is this experiential aspect, connoting intimate, personal participation in or appropriation of that which is known, which distinguishes the biblical understanding of knowing from that most common today. Biblically, speculative and theoretical "knowledge," the mere accumulation of information, is not true knowledge. "Truth" is known only when it is appropriated and obeyed.

Appreciating the biblical understanding of knowing affords insight regarding the place of information in our training programmes. Information is not viewed as inherently valuable; rather its value lies in its capacitating effect—what it enables us to do or the effect God produces through it in our lives. Thus, priority should be given to the application of information taught. Bible truths should be appropriated and obeyed; other truths should be studied for their implications for life and ministry, as well.

Skills training is central to the task of missionary training centres. Research on skills-learning indicates a multi-step approach to training is most effective (Gagné 1985:212-216). Initial instruction should include step-by-step explanation of the skill, specifying those qualities which discriminate appropriate and inappropriate performance. Instruction becomes meaningful when followed by expert demonstration, alternating entire-skill and step-by-step performance. Trainees typically acquire competence only through repeated practice with expert feedback. Interestingly, mental practice (thinking through the steps required and imagining performance) often positively supplements real practice in skill development. To develop expertise after a skill is acquired, trainees must reflect on their performance, focusing on refinements or alternative procedures which can achieve or exceed requisite standards. Trainers should consider the implications of these techniques for skill instruction in the missionary training centre.

Character qualities represent the most fundamental yet the most challenging task of the missionary trainer. Ultimately, the missionary's own life is her or his most powerful message to those who need Christ. Perhaps this is the reason the large majority of biblical standards for spiritual leadership are character qualities.

Training in Christian character must begin with living models. Trainers may be reluctant to say with Paul, "Follow my example, as I follow the example of Christ" (1 Cor 11:1), yet it is demonstration of Christian virtues in daily life, relationships, and ministry which trainees need most.

It is significant, however, how often Jesus taught on godly character. The Sermon on the Mount (Mt 5-7) is an extended discourse on character, and Jesus' condemnation of Jewish religious leaders primarily centred on hypocrisy—a discontinuity between teaching and character (Mt 23; see especially v 2). The ultimate revelation of God was not in prophetic pronouncements but in incarnation (Heb 1:1-2). Nevertheless, even the incarnate Christ had to interpret the significance of his person and ministry (Jn 4:25-26; Lk 24:44-48). If modelling is to have its full training effect, it must be wedded with instruction and intentional, guided reflection on the character qualities modelled.

6. The **ultimate goal** of missionary training—the continuing growth of the trainee.

Growth of the trainee is the ultimate goal—and the ultimate test—of training. Growth differs from change in that growth is defined by its goal. Specifically, missionary training aims at growth in Christ-likeness and growth in ministry effectiveness. God intentionally facilitates growth in his people through the grace he extends, through the active ministry of the indwelling Holy Spirit, and through the power of his Word.

Whereas some training leads to dependency, the effect of training for growth is empowerment. It enables trainees to "take a large view," to appreciate alternative perspectives, customs, and mores. It equips trainees to identify and critique assumptions and values. It prepares trainees to tolerate ambiguity when life experiences do not "make sense." It provides trainees with the capacity to identify sources of information and wisdom, so they can continue learning and growing. It expands trainees' ability to think creatively and to envision alternative models of thought and action. And it develops trainees' capacity to build consensus.

In these six areas, at least—the specific goals, the context, the structure, the learner, the types of learning, and the ultimate goal of missionary training—the programme developer and the training staff need to clarify foundational commitments. The evidence identified in this section, together with any other relevant evidence—biblical, educational, or cultural—should be considered carefully so that the commitments which guide training decisions are appropriately grounded.[8] Furthermore, commitments once made should not be immune from reconsideration. As new evidence surfaces, trainers must be prepared to reexamine their guiding commitments. Ultimately, integrity is defined not in fidelity to commitments embraced at one point in time, but in confidence in the creator-God of truth and in obedience to the totality of his revelation, in Scripture and in nature.

Programme Development
Is a Participative Process

Observation of ministry training programmes around the world indicates that many programme developers, indeed, have clarified and owned their commitments in several of the areas indicated above. In some cases this has been done deliberately and systematically; in other cases commitments have evolved in the midst of programme operation. A few programme developers have studied

---

8. It is assumed that evangelical missionary trainers will not permit educational or cultural evidence to displace clear biblical teaching.

educational research and theory, collecting mountains of data on which to ground their commitments, while others root their commitments in their own observations and experience. Unfortunately, however, very few developers of ministry training programmes have realised the importance of drawing their colleagues—the training staff of their Bible schools and missionary training centres—into dialogue on the commitments which shape training.

Education is a values-laden activity. Whenever we teach or train, we act out our values in innumerable ways, but principally through the ways we approach our task, the ways we handle our lesson materials, and the ways we relate to learners. When a training staff has not collectively examined their training commitments, diverse assumptions and values are inevitable. At the very least, this produces dissonance for trainees, as they receive divergent, sometimes conflicting messages from different trainers. At the worst, trainers who have not owned commitments on which the programme is founded will subvert the official curriculum, intentionally or unintentionally, by promoting their own values. Clearly, if a training programme is to attain coherence, maximising its training effectiveness, the training staff should be united regarding the purposes of the programme and the commitments which guide its implementation. This only can be achieved through deliberate and focused dialogue.

It has been wisely observed that curriculum development (and, we might add, programme development) is a mixture of art and politics (Huebner 1975). Programme development is an art in that it requires creativity. New challenges constantly are encountered. Prior experience and available information may not indicate the most productive path ahead. There is also the challenge of lifting training to new and higher levels of effectiveness. Programme developers must draw on their professionally informed, God-given creativity to meet these challenges. Programme development is an art!

On the other hand, programme development also is politics. Often in our nations, politics is a highly charged, overtly manipulative power struggle. Programme development may devolve to that level, but that is not what is intended here. Rather, programme development is politics in the sense that it builds on shared—and thus, negotiated—values. Like the nation, the city, or the village, coherence and strength must be grounded in a community of shared values. Our greatest political leaders understand this and seek to build consensus on issues of critical importance to the communities which they lead. It is in negotiating values and commitments toward consensus that programme development is politics.

Building consensus on training commitments within one's own training staff may be the programme developer's most important task. To do this effectively, the programme developer first must be clear about his or her own commitments. One would be foolish to lead the training staff blindly into discussion of issues which are unconsidered. The programme developer should be prepared to articulate his or her convictions and to marshal the evidence which justifies them.

On the other hand, it is essential that the programme developer be open to new evidence which surfaces in the course of discussion and be willing to make whatever adjustments are indicated. The programme developer also must be clear—and must communicate explicitly to the training staff—that his or her only non-negotiable loyalties are to God and to truth; everything else is open to discussion and will be resolved on the basis of a collective under-standing of the best evidence available.[9]

Perhaps the greatest impediment to building consensus on our training commitments is the time and effort required. Almost anything is easier than identifying the assumptions and values which shape our training programmes, collecting evidence which bears on those issues, and dialoguing our way through to shared understandings and commitments. Nevertheless, nothing else is so productive in bringing coherence and focus to a training pro-gramme. Simply put, building consensus on training commit-ments is worth the effort!

---

9. One of the greatest tests the programme developer will face is her or his ability to be persuasive without becoming authoritarian, making the case for her or his own convictions, yet graciously yielding when the evidence itself or collective judgment indicates otherwise.

Guidelines for Consensus Building

We close this chapter with nine practical guidelines for building consensus. These guidelines come from our own experience with consensus building in a variety of educational settings, as well as from the experience of others (Elmer 1993; Fisher and Ury 1991).

1. Believe that consensus is attainable.

Unless the programme developer believes unshakably that consensus can be built, the project is doomed from the outset. Whenever differences of perspective polarise into opposing camps, temptation is strong to impose resolution by resorting to power strategies. The inevitable result is a staff fractured into winners and losers. (Western "parliamentary procedure" is specifically crafted to achieve this effect!) It is impossible to have programmatic unity, cohesion, and focus with a fractured staff. We must strenuously avoid win-lose strategies, opting instead for win-win resolutions which protect the values and concerns of all parties. Ultimately, win-win resolutions are essential because relationships are valued.[10]

2. Respect participants, their values and their opinions.

Because God created people in his own image and because he loves people, we also value them and relate to them with respect. This means we do not demean or ridicule others or their perspectives.

Our common commitment to biblical authority provides a network of shared values which makes it easy for Christian training programme developers to affirm and support their training staff. Even when differences surface, issues can be addressed without questioning a staff member's most fundamental convic-

---

10. If any individual holds to commitments so tightly that no consideration is given to contrary evidence, biblical or natural, or to the concerns and values of others, indeed, negotiation may be impossible. When the situation is handled wisely, however, in keeping with the guidelines offered here, we have never encountered a case where Christian colleagues refused to work together. If that were to occur and if the opposing staff are unresponsive to godly counsel, it seems obvious that personnel changes are needed to restore unity to the training programme.

tions. Nevertheless, examining assumptions is threatening to those who have invested much of their lives and resources pursuing particular activities. The programme developer will be wise to communicate respect, to approach the examination of assumptions and values with sensitivity, and steadfastly to rebuff all temptations toward a posture of power.

3.   Identify common ground and work forward.

Perhaps the reason we are not successful more often in our attempts to build consensus relates to our starting point. If we begin with programmes and policies, differences may quickly become polarised, and consensus may be unattainable. The only consistent and effective way to build consensus is to begin from a point of agreement, not from difference. If we believe common ground has been established, then differences emerge, we should recognise immediately that even more fundamental assumptions and values must be explored. Only by establishing a foundation of true agreement, then building forward, can consensus on commitments and their programmatic implementation be forged.

In our experience, we have found that it is best to begin with the Bible. Evangelical ministry trainers all confess allegiance to the Word of God as authoritative for faith and practice. This, then, is our ultimate "common ground." When we begin from educational theories or programme proposals, we inevitably encounter differences and resistance. When we begin from the Bible, identifying doctrines and examples which reflect on the issues at hand, and then examine educational assumptions and proposals on the basis of biblical truths, achieving consensus is not difficult. We would commend this procedure to all training programme developers.

4.   Listen to values and feelings rather than words.

A second impediment to consensus building is exclusive attention to the statements and rationale of those in dialogue. This may seem surprising, since respect for one another would seem to imply respect for what others say. It is important to recognise, however, that our assumptions and values often skew our discussions in unexpected ways. This especially is true when the issues in view are perceived to be fundamental or are ones in which we are heavily invested. When someone appears adamant or when strongly stated cases are put forth in the midst of dialogue, it is useful to explore the sub-text of assumptions and values which underlie these feelings and expressions. This is not to suggest that statements and supporting reasons can be ignored; of course not! If differences are more fundamental, however, it is unlikely that debating more superficial issues will produce understanding.

When it appears that underlying differences exist, it still is important to attend to the ways in which concerns are expressed. Sometimes discussion is frustrated by terms or words which hold powerful meanings or associations for one party. The wise programme developer will quickly identify and isolate "loaded words" and will rephrase the terms of discussion to focus on issues, rather than language.

5.   Constantly verify your understanding.

Others recognise that we have heard them when we restate to them the concerns or observations which they have expressed. It is especially helpful if our restatement focuses even more sharply on the issue they have addressed. Likewise, when we attempt to hear the sub-text of assumptions and values underlying someone's discussion, it is especially important that we frequently verify our perceptions. We might say, "It seems to me that this is important to you because.... Is that a fair statement?" Even when our perceptions are mistaken, such questions often are effective in moving the locus of discussion to a deeper level.

6.   Gently test feelings, assumptions, and values, biblically and empirically.

Consensus is not the ultimate goal; truth is. Harmony is important, but not at the expense of training effectiveness. When genuine common ground has been established and differences emerge in the course of discussion, the bases for these differences must be submitted to biblical and evidential tests. If all parties genuinely desire what is best for the church of Jesus Christ, for world evangelisation, and for equipping trainees as effective ministers, differences can be sorted out. God is not confused, his Word does not set conflicting standards, and the facts found in God's creation, rightly perceived, do not contradict his Word. When pertinent evidence is collected and prayerfully, logically considered, agreement is possible. This is the process by which consensus is forged.

7.   *Explore alternative means to guard appropriate values.*

Even when assumptions and commitments are shared, differences in personal priorities may give rise to hesitation or concern regarding specific programme proposals. Often the underlying values are legitimate. At that point the programme developer must assist the group in identifying alternative courses of action which will promote the intended agenda, yet will protect the values of the concerned member.

Often this is a critical point in consensus building. With fundamental agreement already attained, it is tempting to ignore concerns about details of implementation. To appreciate the significance of the situation, however, it must be viewed in larger context. The real issue is not the importance or unimportance of the concern raised; rather, it is the programme developer's commitment to respect every member of the training team and to assure that true consensus is achieved. Although such concerns often surface when the group is tired and ready for a break—i.e., when creativity and perhaps patience are in short supply—protection of the concerned member's interests will do more to cement mutual commitment within the group than anything else the programme developer can do.

8.   *Elicit and record mutual confirmation of intermediate agreements.*

When a consensus building project is large, as when commitments are initially established to guide development of a training programme, it is useful to document the process. Usually it is not helpful to record discussion, but when the programme developer senses that consensus has been established in a specific area, that should be noted. Typically the programme developer will state the points of agreement, as he or she understands them, then will ask each member of the group to respond with affirmation or further clarification. When unanimous concurrence is affirmed, this will provide closure for that phase of the discussion; the group is free to move ahead to consider new issues. When documented, affirmation of consensus also provides a record for group members to consult if any differences later arise over the specific understandings which were adopted.

9. Be patient and persistent.

Consensus building is a time-consuming, patience-testing task. The only rational motivation for choosing to develop a programme on consensus-based commitments is because it is right. Consensus building is right theologically; it treats colleagues with the respect they are due as fellow-bearers of God's image. Consensus building is right epistemologically; it recognises that truth is unified in God and that humans can recognise truth through rational processes. Consensus building is right organisationally; it enables a training group to focus its diverse energies and resources for maximum effectiveness. And consensus building is right educationally; by modelling unity in diversity, trainers empower trainees to become consensus builders in their own ministries.

Patience and persistence are especially needed when areas of disagreement seem intractable. A realistic rule of thumb is to accept disagreement only in minor details, and then reluctantly. Don't settle for 90% agreement if 98% is possible. On the other hand, a programme developer will avoid disappointment and despair by bearing in mind that humans are fallen creatures. Even mature Christians at times evidence the effects of sin on their logical processes. With experience, programme developers will learn to sense when it is time to press for consensus in greater detail and when it is time to accept the level of consensus which has been achieved and move on.

Conclusion

Shared, deliberately chosen commitments, not unexamined assumptions or values, afford the only firm foundation on which to develop programmes for missionary training. In this chapter we have identified six areas in which shared commitments are needed, and we have outlined an approach to building consensus. At the 1994 International Missionary Training Consultants' Seminar, this process was demonstrated.[11] It should be noted, however, that

---

11. The commitments negotiated appear in Appendix A.

the *process* of building consensus potentially is much more significant than specific points that are negotiated. While building consensus on commitments to guide programme decisions, participants also build relationships, understanding, and trust. Programme developers should take care to assure that these potential benefits are not forfeited by reluctance to understand and negotiate.

Chapter 2

Developing an Outcomes Profile

Jonathan Lewis and Robert Ferris

Often curriculum is developed based on the availability of textbooks and other didactic material, plus the availability of an instructor and his or her level of expertise. While this approach works to keep schools or training programmes going, it is less than ideal. Training programme administrators need to have a clear view of what they want to achieve through their training and then organise resources to meet those goals. Seeing the target is fundamental to hitting it!

Traditional ministry training programmes emphasise knowledge transfer. Emphasis is on knowledge which a student is expected to need in ministry. The programme specifies information which students must know and on which they are tested. When well implemented, the cumulative result is a knowledgeable person, certified with a grade, a certificate, or a degree. It is assumed the graduate will be able to draw on this reserve of information once in practice.

In contrast, the best way to approach the development of a sound curriculum is to determine the desired outcomes and then build "backwards" to ascertain all of the resources needed to reach the training goal. When we define outcome goals, we describe the results that can be expected from carrying out a training programme. Then we can plan a curriculum for achieving these results.

The profiling exercise creates a verbal picture—a "profile"—which defines outcome goals in a holistic manner, specifically focusing on the character qualities and skills needed for effectiveness in ministry. If the profile leads to curricula which yield these outcomes, upon completion of the training a "graduate" will have gained the specified level of development in each character and skill area. This is an important shift from concern only with what individuals need to *know* to what they *are* and *can do* as a result of training. In the following pages, we outline the steps and provide a rationale for conducting a profiling exercise oriented specifically to ministry training.

Planning the Profiling Exercise

The purpose of this section is to enable you to utilise the profiling technique in your own institutional training context. This will require some planning and an outline of the procedures to use. First you will need to answer some basic questions:

1. How long does profiling take?

The profiling workshop can fit into one day if it is conducted with a relatively small, homogeneous group (8–14 people) and if it is well organised. When more time is allowed for reflection and dialogue, however, a more complete and satisfying profile can be developed. When the workshop is spread over two or three days, a greater depth will be achieved, and participants generally will become more committed to what is produced. With a large group, the process definitely will take more than one day. The facilitator of a large workshop also should be aware of the work that is needed between group sessions to keep the process running smoothly.

2. Who should be involved?

With appropriate guidance, effective practitioners are best able to identify the qualifications needed for a given role. This would indicate that active missionaries are our most important source of information regarding the qualities and skills missionaries should possess. They should comprise the majority of participants in the profiling exercise.

We also recognise, however, that others need to be involved in the process. A profile is useful only if it is accepted by those who

will apply it to training programmes. Trainers who do not participate in the profiling exercise tend to resist when asked to design
and implement curricular changes based on the resulting profile.
When they are included in the process, however, they are much
more likely to own responsibility for its implementation.

There also are others who have a "stake" in missionary training—mission agency administrators, pastors of sending churches,
and the missionary candidates themselves. All of these comprise
our "stakeholders." Where missionaries are serving national
church constituencies, leaders of the receiving church also are
significant stakeholders.

When conducting a profiling workshop, invite wise and respected members of each stakeholding group to participate. In this
way, a forum is created for missionaries, trainers, mission agency
administrators, sending pastors, and even trainees to join in
determining what kind of missionaries are needed—and, thus,
what qualities and skills a training programme should seek to
develop. This consensus approach is critical in creating commitment to implementation or change in training programmes.

3. What size group should be involved?

The profiling workshops conducted in Latin America and Asia
have been performed with as many as seventy international representatives from many different denominations, mission agencies, and training programmes. While a group this size makes the
profiling exercise more difficult to manage, these workshops over-
came this challenge by dividing into smaller groups for the most
interactive phases. This required that a number of small group
coordinators be selected and oriented before the workshops. These
coordinators also functioned as a single "small group" at points
when complexity made it impractical to proceed with either the
large group or the separate small groups. Throughout this chapter,
suggestions are provided for those responsible for facilitating the
profiling process with a large group.

Ideally, a missionary profile should be developed by a small
group that represents a single mission, its training unit, and
representative stakeholders. Under these circumstances, all those
affected can be involved without unnecessarily complicating the
management of the process by the large size of the group. When

done in this way, cohesion is lent to the subsequent curriculum development and implementation phases.

4.   Who should facilitate the process?

The profiling workshop is led by a facilitator whose responsibilities include managing the time and agenda, eliciting participation from all, and assuring that the evolving profile results in a completed document. It always is helpful to share this responsibility with someone else who understands the process. There may be times when the group dynamic will be broken or otherwise impeded if the facilitator has no assistant.

It is important for facilitators to understand their role thoroughly. They do not function as experts on missionary training (though they may be), but as facilitators who assure that the profiling process is carried out smoothly and with integrity. They must not be domineering, but rather elicit active participation from all members. Ideally, the workshop facilitator is not a stakeholder of the institution and thus is freed from any need, personal or official, to influence the outcome of the process. The facilitator must manage the whole process, including the selection and training of small group coordinators.

As mentioned previously, when a profiling exercise is conducted with a large group, a coordinator will be needed for each small group. Coordinators should be selected early, preferably before the larger group is convened. A primary consideration in selection is their ability to facilitate group interaction. In many cultures younger persons may perform best for a number of reasons. They quickly capture the concept of engaging group members in the process, they are less likely to be authoritarian, and they usually exhibit the mental agility needed to keep the group focused on an assigned task. On the other hand, younger persons may be less experienced at building consensus from divergent viewpoints. This suggests a critical focus when preparing group coordinators.

5.   Where should a profiling workshop be held?

The usual location for a profiling workshop is a classroom or conference facility. The room should have a blank wall where cards listing missionary qualifications can be posted. If the group is small, seating should be arranged in a circle or semi-circle. Moveable seating is important for a large group. Good lighting, ventilation, and acoustics also are important.

6. *What is needed to conduct the sessions?*

There are several simple items that are necessary to conduct the workshop. These include cards or pieces of paper and some way to stick them on the wall. Cards can be waxed on the back (so they will adhere to a surface), or a non-greasy sticky putty can be used. (Tape is not recommended because it might damage the wall paint.) An easel with blank paper, a large chalkboard, or an overhead projector may be used at some points in the exercise, if available. Narrow-tipped marking pens also are useful.

Conducting the Profiling Workshop

In order to help you conduct the profiling workshop, we have listed each phase of the exercise, step by step. If you have never conducted a profiling exercise, you may want to rehearse these steps. It will give you a feel for timing and other factors critical to the success of the exercise. You don't want to disappoint participants by transmitting confusion and lack of personal understanding of the steps in developing a missionary profile.

The facilitator will lead the workshop group through six phases:
- *Phase 1* – Orientation to the process.
- *Phase 2* – Identify the type of missionary to be profiled and create a job description.
- *Phase 3* – Identify the *general areas* of character and ministry-skill qualifications.
- *Phase 4* – Identify *specific* qualities and competencies.
- *Phase 5* – Create the profile chart.
- *Phase 6* – Review and endorse the profile chart.

When your workshop group is small (8–14 persons), each of the above phases will be carried out with the whole group. If the workshop is large (more than 14 people), trained coordinators will be needed to lead small groups in Phases 1 and 4.[1]

Phase 1 – Orientation

The facilitator should create a sense of anticipation about the profiling process. It is important for participants to know why they are involved in the workshop and what outcome is expected. Questions and discussion should be encouraged so that everyone understands what is expected of them during the hours (or days) of the workshop. Schedules and other administrative matters should be explained. Questions regarding the process should be answered before the brainstorming session begins.

Workshop participants should be helped to view one another as colleagues, working toward a common goal. When participants do not know each other, they should be given opportunity to introduce themselves. It may be valuable to conduct an "ice breaker," an activity which helps the group to relax and to begin to participate. There are many ways to do this, but an easy way is to ask each person to share a "nick-name" they have (or have had) and how they received it. These (or first names) should be written

---

1. In a large group the work may be divided as follows:
   - *Pre-session* – Anticipate the number of small groups which will be needed. Recruit and train one coordinator for each small group. The coordinators will also function as a group in Phases 2, 4, and 5.
   - *Phase 1* – Facilitator leads large group; coordinators lead introductions in small groups.
   - *Phase 2* – Facilitator leads coordinator group and presents recommendation to the large group to be adjusted, as needed, and approved.
   - *Phase 3* – Facilitator leads large group.
   - *Phase 4* – Coordinators lead small groups. Coordinator group collates lists generated by the small groups. Facilitator presents the collated list to the large group to be adjusted, as needed, and approved.
   - *Phase 5* – Facilitator leads coordinator group.
   - *Phase 6* – Facilitator leads large group.

on cards which are visible to the group so others can use these names in ensuing discussions. During these introductions the facilitator should highlight the potential contribution of each individual, to encourage all to participate. When a workshop is large, introductions and the ice breaker should be conducted in the small groups.

Setting a Context for Brainstorming

It is unfortunate, but true, that we naturally focus on formal (academic) and pragmatic (skill) factors when identifying qualifications for any role. A useful technique for establishing biblical perspective regarding ministry (including missionary) qualifications is to ask participants to review 1 Timothy 3:1-7, 2 Timothy 2:24-25, and Titus 1:6-9, three passages which describe the qualifications of a church leader. Using a chalkboard or overhead projector, make three parallel columns. Figure 2:1 shows how these columns should be headed.

A Church Leader Should Know (Knowledge)	A Church Leader Should Be Able To (Skills)	A Church Leader Should Be (Character Qualities)

Figure 2:1. Sample Chart for Identifying
Qualifications of a Church Leader

As participants read through the listed passages, invite them to identify the qualifications Paul (under the inspiration of the Holy Spirit) lists for a church leader. As each qualification is noted, request the person who named it to indicate in which column it should be entered. (Since there is some duplication among these lists, it is not necessary to reproduce that duplication in the chart.)

This exercise usually takes only about fifteen minutes, but it may precipitate a longer discussion. Participants quickly will recognise that most New Testament qualifications fall into the third column, "Character Qualities." "Knowledge" is almost unmentioned in these passages. If participants have not seen this before, it will challenge their assumptions about priorities in ministry training.

A common question relates to the scant notice given to "knowledge" qualifications. It would be easy (but dangerous!) to conclude that knowledge is unimportant in spiritual leadership. A more insightful perspective recognises that knowledge is given by God, not as an end of itself (that's when "knowledge puffs up"), but as a means toward holiness and ministry. Knowledge is important because of the way God uses it to shape our lives and the way he enables us to use it in the lives of others. Thus, God develops the many listed "character qualities" in us when we fill our minds and hearts with his Word and when we obey it. This helps us understand the Bible's emphasis on "obeying the truth."

Other knowledge is essential to effective skills in ministry. Every skill assumes (or requires) certain knowledge. A medical doctor must know a great deal about the human body, diseases, and medicines in order to know how to treat patients. A launderer must know about the characteristics of fabrics, dyes, and stains in order to know how to remove a spot without destroying the garment. Likewise, a Christian must know God's Word before she or he can know how to obey it or teach others to do so.

Yet, "to know" is not the same as "to know how." A basic understanding of social or cultural standards is necessary to develop one's skills in communication, witness, and ministry. One can learn cultural standards, however, without learning how to communicate or witness effectively. All of us also "know" standards of our own culture even though we may have difficulty articulating them. This warns us not to equate "knowledge" with expression.

Knowledge typically is valued for one of two reasons. Sometimes knowledge is valued because it affords prestige or power. Elitism and demagoguery are inconsistent, however, with Christian virtues.

Knowledge also may be valued for its usefulness. It enables us to be or to do what otherwise is impossible—note the illustrations of the medical doctor and the launderer, above. Thus, knowledge has instrumental value. (This is not to disparage a lively curiosity, but only to acknowledge that satisfying curiosities is not the purpose of most training programmes.)

Recognising the instrumental value of knowledge—nourishing holiness and enabling ministry—helps us understand the importance of "knowledge" qualifications for ministry. Understanding that the role and value of knowledge is fundamentally instrumental, however, also clarifies why training programme developers do well first to focus on character qualities ("being" goals) and ministry skills ("doing" goals), then allow these to help sort out what knowledge is required for effective missionary service. (These insights will shape our procedure in Phase 3 and in the following chapter.)

As soon as participants have recognised the significance of this study of biblical qualifications for church leadership, it is time to move on. Many participants will continue to reflect on this exercise and its implications for ministry (including missionary) training. Continued discussion during break times or meal times can be encouraged, but it is important to move ahead with identifying missionary qualifications if the larger task of profiling is to be achieved.

Phase 2 – Identify the Type of Missionaries Needed

Simple as it may seem, specifically identifying the type of missionaries to be trained is vital to this process. While the title "missionary" is easily accepted in the evangelical community, it means many things to many people.

There are at least four dimensions on which it is useful to clarify the type of missionaries to be trained (list the following on a chalkboard, flip chart, or overhead transparency):

- *Cultural distance:* Will mission work be concentrated among people of the same culture as the missionaries, of a culture near to that of the missionaries, or of a remote or very different culture from that of the missionaries?
- *Specific ministry:* Will missionaries primarily be involved in evangelism and church-planting or in some form of specialised ministry (literature, radio, medical, mercy ministries, education, etc.)?
- *Financial support:* Will missionaries be mission supported or self-supported (i.e., "tentmakers")?

- *Term of service:* Will missionaries be expected to serve for their full career, for a limited term (two to six years), or for a short term (less than two years)?

Specifying the type of missionary to be trained in no way establishes that type of missionary as more significant than any other. The New Testament teaches that within the body of Christ are many members, each with his or her own role and contribution. What is essential to the health of the body is the faithful fulfillment of each member's role.

Neither does identification of one type of missionary to be trained imply that only one type is needed in any particular region or field. Rather, it defines the limits of this specific profiling exercise. If several types of missionaries are needed, individual profiles should be developed for each one. To avoid duplication of effort, a core set of characteristics may be identified which are common to all types. Then build upon this core set to create specific profiles for diverse missionary roles.

In groups where several training goals are represented, it is important for participants to recognise that identifying one type of missionary for profiling does not imply that other types of ministry are less important, nor does it preclude focus on another type of missionary in a subsequent profiling exercise. If these things are made clear, consensus usually develops rather quickly, even in a large group. Nevertheless, it is important that participants agree on the type of missionary they are profiling. When consensus has been reached, the type of missionary is identified with a title as in Figure 2:2.

Type of Missionary to Be Trained
Mission-supported, career, cross-cultural church planter

Figure 2:2

Describing the Missionary Type

Once a specific type of missionary has been identified as the focus of the profiling exercise, it is useful to create a definition of who the missionary is and what he or she does. The original studies conducted with this process assumed that the type of missionary to be profiled is a career (long-term), cross-cultural church planter. Because the group was diverse, we used Matthew 28:18-20 as the basis of our definition. Participants agreed on a definition like the one in Figure 2:3.

Definition of a Cross-Cultural Church Planting Missionary

Cross-cultural church planting missionaries are messengers sent by their respective churches to places where there is no Christian witness. They live an exemplary life and communicate the gospel in ways their new neighbours can understand. Their aim is to see conversions to Jesus Christ. They teach believers to obey all of Christ's commandments. The final goal of their missionary activity is a body of obedient Christian disciples who are able to carry on the work of evangelism and discipleship among their own people and who are eager and able to reach other peoples also.

Figure 2:3

Phase 3 – Identify the General Areas of Qualifications

The task before the group is to make a list of major areas of qualification needed for effective missionary service. Note that the distinction between Phase 3 and Phase 4 is one of degree rather than kind. Phase 3 identifies broad categories; Phase 4 will detail specific qualifications within these categories. This two-step procedure facilitates analysis. (The process quickly loses focus if we become specific too soon or if we fail to discriminate between broad categories and specific qualifications.) It is important, at this point, that participants understand their task and discipline themselves to think in broad categories.

The most efficient way to make this list is to conduct a "green light" or "brainstorming" session. Suggestions are taken from the group and written on cards, a chalkboard, or an overhead transparency. Again, provide separate columns for "Character Areas" and "Skill Areas."[2] The assistant should list areas proposed by the

---

2. As noted in Phase 1, "knowledge" is not considered at this time, since critical knowledge will contribute toward—and is best identified in terms of—character or skill qualifications. Knowledge qualifications, although omitted from the profile, will be a major consideration at the point of curriculum development.

group, while the facilitator works to elicit additional responses. Do not pause to discuss any of the suggestions at this time.

This phase draws on the experience of participants to identify qualification areas.[3] A question like one of the following may help participants begin identifying qualification areas:

- What qualities and skills enable you to be an effective church planting missionary?
- What qualities and skills distinguish your most effective church planting missionaries?

The result of the "green light" session should be a list of character qualities and skills like the one in Figure 2:4. (Note, however, that this example is deliberately incomplete so participants will not be tempted simply to copy someone else's list of qualification areas.)

Character Qualities	Skills
• Commitment to the Bible • Missionary "heart" • Honours his or her parents • Marriage reflects the relationship of Christ to his church • Lovingly trains children in godliness • Children behave and obey • … and several more	• Language and communication • Culture learning and adaptation • Interpersonal relationships • Evangelism and follow-up • … and several more

Figure 2:4. Sample List of Missionary Qualifications

Insights derived from the study of biblical qualifications (Phase 1) and the definition of the type of missionary needed (Phase 2) may suggest qualification areas to be included in these lists. They also should be used to check that no significant qualification areas have been overlooked in the "green light" session.

---

3. It is important to bear in mind that the participants' experience in ministry is the primary resource and focus of the "green light" session. The task is not to exegete the biblical qualifications or our "definition" of the type of missionary to be trained. Throughout the "green light" session, the facilitator should assure that focus is kept on characteristics of effective missionary models.

When no more suggestions are forthcoming,[4] the facilitator begins to work with the group to consolidate the list into distinct areas of training. Where several areas seem to overlap, they may be condensed into a single area (see Figure 2:5). Occasionally, a suggestion may encompass too much and can be divided into more than one discrete area.

Listed Areas	Condensed Area
• Honours his or her parents • Marriage reflects the relationship of Christ to his church • Lovingly trains children in godliness • Children behave and obey	• Christian family life

Figure 2:5. Consolidating Qualification Areas into Distinct Areas of Training

Typically, a useful list will identify eight to twelve areas of character qualities and a similar number of skill competencies. If your lists exceed these limits, you probably would do well to invest more time in looking for broader categories which enable you to consolidate your list even more. The final result will be a list of clearly identified areas for which future practitioners will need training.

Review and Endorse the List of Qualification Areas

Whether the final list of qualification areas is developed by the group as a whole or by the coordinator group, it is important that all participants have an opportunity to review the list and express concurrence that the areas they consider important have been included. To proceed in the profiling process is not wise if even a few participants are dissatisfied with the list of qualification areas.

It is best at this point to solicit vocal statements of support—or residual concerns—from all participants. If the facilitator has been

---

4. In a large group setting, there is a point when the identification of training areas may become counter-productive as people argue different perspectives. It is advisable to break off the exercise at this point and continue the work of revising the list of areas with the coordinator group.

attentive to comments and concerns expressed during the process of consolidation, these endorsements usually are quickly and candidly expressed.

Phase 4 – Identify Specific Missionary Qualities and Competencies

This is the heart of the process. For each character and skill area, specific character qualities or skill competencies must be identified and articulated in succinct statements of observable behaviour. Ultimately, these will be arranged in a profile chart with the general areas in a vertical row on the left and the qualification statements extending in horizontal rows to the right from each area.[5] This phase involves four distinct steps:

1. *Choose a qualification area to work on.*

There is no specific order in which the identified qualification areas need to be treated. One which seems simple and straightforward may be best to start with. Each area may take an hour or more to discuss.[6]

2. *Conduct a "green light" session.*

Encourage everyone in the group to think of specific qualities or skills which an effective missionary needs in the qualification area selected.[7] This is a similar exercise to that conducted for identifying the general areas, but now the focus is on specific qualities and skills that will be required in that area. Figure 2:6

---

5. Due to the small page size of this book and the difficulty in reading columns of tiny print, this format has been modified in most of the examples in this manual.

6. When a large group has been divided into smaller groups and time is limited (perhaps to three or four hours), the areas may be divided among the groups as well. When this is done, it is best to assign each area to two or three small groups in different combinations. Thus, qualities or competencies for each area will be identified by more than one group.

7. In some cultural contexts, it may be more appropriate to open up the discussion to all the identified areas. As each quality and competency is discussed, list it in the appropriate area.

General Area	Specific Characteristics		
Interpersonal relations	Applies biblical principles to relationships	Listens to others and responds appropriately	Manages interpersonal conflict well

**Figure 2:6. Identifying Specific Qualities
and Skills Required for Each General Area**

illustrates a few of the characteristics described under the general area of "Interpersonal Relationships" in the original study.

It is best to "brainstorm" and try to cover the entire area first, rather than discuss each quality or skill as it is suggested. Encourage participation until no more suggestions are forthcoming. It is not unusual for this original list to have twenty or twenty-five suggestions for a single qualification area.

3. *Discuss the qualities and competencies listed.*

Once a fairly comprehensive list of specific characteristics has been compiled, begin discussing the items to determine their appropriateness to the area. Some items may be compressed into one. Each item should be expressed in succinct statements of measurable or observable behaviour. This will require the use of a verb, preferably an action verb. All items need to be observable and/or measurable; without a verb, this is impossible. Figure 2:7 illustrates this principle.

Under the character area "Church Related," a qualification may be identified:

> *Knows how to inform the church
> on the missionary task.*

This competency might be stated more strongly as:

> *Successfully informs the church
> about mission efforts.*

This rewording moves the qualification from a passive skill to an activity which demonstrates the skill.

**Figure 2:7. Expressing Competencies in Terms
of Measurable and/or Observable Behaviours**

As you examine each item, you will want to ask: Is this observable? If so, how? Asking these questions will help the group sharpen each item in such a way that it will be useful in the eventual design of a curriculum which recognises or develops the quality or skill.

It is important to note that most character qualities will be difficult to articulate in directly observable terms, but specific behaviours which indicate a presence of these traits may be more easily identified. ("By their fruit you will know them.") The item "Is Christ-like in character" is difficult to observe, but behaviours reflecting Christ-likeness, such as "Is considerate of others" or "Serves others readily," are more specific and observable. A skillful facilitator or coordinator will help the group come up with the right verb and phrasing for each item.

The product of this phase should be a list of succinct statements under each general qualification area which expresses, in terms of observable characteristics, what qualities or skills are required for effective missionary service.[8] Each area may have up to eight or ten of these succinct statements. If there are many more, however, it is likely the area is too broad and, under analysis, a natural sub-division will be apparent.

4.   Review lists of qualities and competencies.

Once the specific qualities and competencies for all the areas have been identified and listed, they should be reviewed together to assure appropriate completeness. A quality or competency might be removed from an area if duplication occurs, or it may be reworded to express a more specific concept. Likewise, qualities or competencies which have been overlooked may come to light.

---

8. When overlapping lists are created by small groups, the facilitator and the coordinator group will need to collate the individual lists into one single list reflecting the complementary efforts of the larger group. Some items may need to be reworded to achieve internal consistency. It is important to afford an opportunity for all large group members to review and (as necessary) to revise the collated list, although this may be deferred until completion of Phase 5.

Phase 5 – Create the Profile Chart

Once the qualities and competencies for each area are identified, attempt to order or prioritise them. Skill competencies should be arranged in sequential order of development. Character qualities rarely admit to sequential ordering, yet broad priorities usually are recognisable within character areas—some evidences are essential, others are desirable but not essential, etc. Sequential ordering may have significance only for "clusters" (i.e., several evidences appear to bear equal importance), rather than for individual characteristics. That is fine; high levels of priority definition are not required. This exercise is only intended to facilitate production, review, and elaboration of the profile chart.[9]

As each skill or character area is considered in turn, draw a horizontal line with a vertical mark near its mid-point, as in Figure 2:8. Let the vertical mark represent minimal qualification for entrance into field ministry. The line extending to the right will represent goals for pre-field missionary training, while the line to the left will represent goals for in-ministry professional development.

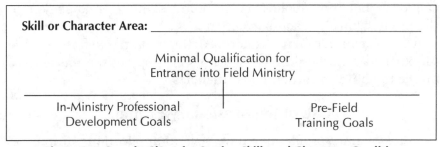

Skill or Character Area: _____

Minimal Qualification for
Entrance into Field Ministry

In-Ministry Professional   Pre-Field
Development Goals   Training Goals

Figure 2:8. Sample Chart for Sorting Skills and Character Qualities

Sort the qualifications listed into these two categories. Next, prioritise qualifications within these categories, from left to right along the line drawn. Order character qualities in ascending order of priority, and skill competencies in descending order of complexity. Thus, the most basic quality or competence for each area will

---

9. If the group is large, ranking of qualifications and creation of the profile chart may be delegated to the coordinator group.

appear at the right end of the line, with the highest or most developed evidence of each area indicated on the left end.

To create the profile chart, list character and skill areas vertically, at the left side of the work space. Array the prioritised list of qualifications for each area immediately to the right of the area name. This likely will require adjusting the placement of the "minimal qualifications" (vertical) marker. That is not a problem. Some areas may consist largely of "minimal qualifications," in which case the marker will be shifted to the left. Other areas may present few minimal qualifications but identify several levels of professionalism to be developed in ministry. In these areas the marker will shift to the right. Be certain, however, that the "minimal qualifications" marker is clearly indicated on the profile chart. See Appendices B, C, D, and E for sample profiles we have developed.

Phase 6 – Review and Endorse the Profile Chart

The completed profile chart should be reviewed by the practitioner-participants. Any modifications called for should be made to the satisfaction of the group as a whole.[10] Again, it is useful to call for verbal or symbolic (e.g., standing, signing) endorsement of the profile chart by each participant.

Once the profile chart is endorsed, the profiling exercise is over. All participants should receive a finished copy of the missionary profile to share with their constituencies.

Use of the Missionary Profile

A missionary profile may have several applications. It may be employed in the internal evaluation of existing missionary training programmes. By comparing current outcomes with those listed in the profile, programmes can determine whether they are "on course" and where to make appropriate adjustments.

A missionary profile also may be used by candidates, pastors, mission administrators, and trainers to evaluate a candidate's

---

10. When the size of the group dictates that the qualification lists created in small groups be collated, ranked, and charted by the coordinator group, it is essential that the resulting profile chart be submitted to all participants for review and adjustment, as needed.

readiness for mission work at each stage of his/her development. Each item can be rated by those involved in the evaluation and expectations clarified in terms of standards to be achieved.

When developing individualised curricula, participants should set a target level of function, or "standard of achievement," for each qualification. Some standards regarding emotional, spiritual, or other personal traits may need to be based on the subjective evaluation of trainers or mentors who observe and monitor the candidate's life and ministry over a period of time. Individualised training can then be implemented to address specific strengths and weaknesses.

Finally, a missionary profile may become the basis for developing new missionary training programmes. This is the primary use envisioned in this manual. New missionary training programmes can be organised and implemented to develop the outcomes identified by the profile chart. Translating qualities and competencies into curricula involves developing appropriate learning objectives and teaching-learning strategies.

Conclusion

There seems to be a consistent message received by those who have worked together to develop missionary training profiles: the task is much more complex than it appears at first sight! The formal classroom experience, which traditionally has been emphasised, seems but a small part of the equipping process. For the missionary to function successfully, so much depends on critical character qualities, attitudes, relational skills, and ability for ministry.

The missionary profile affords a means for understanding the scope of this training task. It also provides a ministry-based beginning point for curriculum development and for allocating training responsibilities. Understanding our task gives us greater confidence we can hit the training target.

Chapter 3

Transforming a Profile into Training Goals

Robert Ferris and Lois Fuller

A profile chart sometimes has been referred to as a training "curriculum." While there may be truth in this observation, we do not find this a helpful way to use these terms. Developing a ministry profile is an important first step in designing a training curriculum. The profile enables the programme developer to identify outcome goals. A second critical step entails transforming outcome goals into training goals. Finally, training goals must be translated into programme and lesson plans, including specific learning objectives and training strategies. This chapter will provide guidance for the second of these three steps.

Who should develop training goals?

Like the profiling exercise, determining training goals is best undertaken as a cooperative project, although the participants needed are different. To develop the profile chart, it was necessary to involve persons familiar—preferably by effective, personal experience—with the specific ministry to be profiled. In this step, participants should be pastors of sending churches, mission personnel directors, Bible school deans, and the missionary training centre director—i.e., the persons responsible for missionary training in each of the cooperating organisations.

It is best if the number of trainers who participate in this process is relatively small. At this point, training experience, insight, and expertise are of greater value than broad participation.

43

Six to ten representative and experienced trainers may constitute an ideal group.

Because the group is small and participants bring considerable expertise, the role of the facilitator is less directive than in the profiling exercise. Participants should view themselves as a curriculum development team. The facilitator's responsibilities may be limited to clarifying the task, maintaining orderly progress, and assuring that conclusions are preserved in a form acceptable to all participants.

What is the task?

As indicated above, the immediate task is to transform outcome goals, identified in the ministry profile, into training goals. It is useful to think of this as consisting of one primary task and two subsidiary tasks.

First, trainers must identify knowledge goals. These, with the quality and skill goals identified by practitioners in the profiling step, are the training goals which will guide programme development.

Second, trainers must determine who will be responsible for pursuing each of the training goals. This entails distributing responsibility for training among the members of the training community. It is essential that the responsibilities distributed are owned by those to whom they are entrusted.

Finally, trainers must determine how best to pursue training goals. A reciprocal relationship exists between "who" and "how," so that these two subsidiary tasks often must be taken together.

What do I need to know to direct or to participate in this task?

Participants should be experienced trainers, aware of basic principles of human learning, thoroughly familiar with the potentials and limitations of their own training resources, and able to listen perceptively, to communicate accurately, and to negotiate toward consensus. The purpose of this chapter is to set a context for participative decisions regarding training goals, approaches, and responsibilities.

As in the profiling exercise, it is essential that participants view each other as colleagues, not as adversaries or competitors. Indeed, there is an enemy, but his objective is to confuse and frustrate effective curriculum development. Participants should acknowledge that none of their colleagues in this project share his interests.

Identifying Training Goals

Before proceeding, it is necessary to clarify the distinction between "outcome goals" and "training goals." Outcome goals focus specifically on those qualities which distinguish effective practitioners—who they are and what they are able to do. Training goals look more comprehensively at the training task. Training goals include outcome (i.e., character quality and skill) goals, but they add knowledge goals as well.

Why are training goals important?

The previous chapter described a profiling strategy for identifying outcome goals. At that point we recognised the importance of knowledge but noted that the value of knowledge lies in its instrumental effect. We asked practitioner-participants to defer the question of what trainees need to know, and to focus on identifying what they must be and must be able to do.

For curriculum development to proceed, outcome goals must be transformed into training goals. As noted above, training goals are more comprehensive than outcome goals, since they include knowledge goals.

Training goals also are more holistic than outcome goals. Whereas discussions of qualities and skills may become atomistic, listing one specific skill or quality after another, training goals recognise the interrelatedness of human life and learning. This interrelatedness is viewed not as a problem to be remedied, but as a benefit to be seized and celebrated. Natural links among knowledge, skill, and character goals are noted for reference when distributing training responsibilities or when designing training programmes.

How are "knowledge goals" identified?

The profile chart consists of prioritised lists of character qualities and skill competencies. It is important for the curriculum development team to resist the strong temptation to debate the appropriateness and comprehensiveness of qualities and competencies included on the profile chart. It must be assumed that practitioners know best what qualities and skills are needed and that trainers know best how to train toward those competencies. The integrity of the curriculum development model depends on respecting the contribution of each group.

Knowledge goals may include Bible backgrounds and history; theology; social science theories (i.e., communication theory); languages (verbal and nonverbal); specific geographical, historical, political, or cultural information; etc. Any theory or facts essential to developing or using needed skills, and any information which significantly supports and fosters desired character qualities, may be a knowledge goal.

Knowledge goals will be limited to and disciplined by the qualities and skills listed in the profile chart. The identification of knowledge goals will be accomplished in three phases.

Phase 1 – Identify Knowledge Required for Skill Competencies

It is best to begin the task of identifying knowledge goals by focusing on skill competencies. Start with the "minimal qualifications" for ministry (i.e., those qualifications on the profile chart to the right of the marker), and come back to professional development qualifications as time allows. As the curriculum development team addresses each skill competency, it should ask, "What must a trainee know in order to do this?"

In this question, the most important word is "must." As soon as the issue of "knowledge goals" is opened, generations of intellectual traditions rush in upon us, quickly suggesting long lists of "important" knowledge—often closely parallelling existing curricula.

The issue of traditional curricula is complex. Curriculum developers never can afford to discount information simply because it is part of traditional schooling. We also cannot afford to discount, however, the extent to which our own intellectual traditions powerfully, although unconsciously, shape our concepts of training and ministry. For this reason, it is appropriate to greet each suggested goal with a "hermeneutic of suspicion." "Is it really necessary for a trainee to know this?" we might ask. Or, "Why is this needed? Which skill competency would the trainee be unable to develop or demonstrate without this knowledge?" By testing each suggested knowledge goal against the specified skill goals, the economy and focus of the training curriculum can be assured.

Phase 2 – Identify Knowledge Which Fosters Character Qualities

The relationship between knowledge and character is quite different from the relationship between knowledge and skills. Specific knowledge is essential to development and performance of any skill. Character, in contrast, is not a function of knowledge. Your friends with the greatest integrity (young children, for example) also may be the least educated (i.e., knowledgeable). On the other hand, many have learned by sad experience that the most knowledgeable individuals sometimes are the least trustworthy. This warns us that asking "What must a trainee know to be like this?" is not a useful way to proceed when identifying knowledge goals related to character qualities.

It often is said that character qualities are "better caught than taught," that is, they are best taught by reflection on living models. Nevertheless, knowledge of the Scriptures is vital. The Scriptures teach us God's standards for holy living and record the life and ministry of Jesus Christ, our ultimate example. Paul reminds us that the Old Testament histories are "written for our instruction" (1 Cor 10:6, 11). Furthermore, God uses his Word as a channel to bring his grace into our lives. Knowledge of historical models of godly character, as in the stories of saints and martyrs or in missionary biographies, also is useful. Thus, for each character quality listed, ask, "What knowledge is needed to reprove, to instruct, or to foster the development of this quality?"

Again, the critical term is "needed." This is not the time to smuggle into the curriculum areas of personal or professional interest. This is not an opportunity to justify intellectual traditions or academic disciplines in which we are vested. Knowledge goals should relate directly to character qualities. As with skill competencies, priority should be assigned to identifying knowledge goals related to minimal character qualifications. Also as before, when examining suggested knowledge goals, we should employ a "hermeneutic of suspicion."

Focusing on the instrumental quality of knowledge, identified in the previous chapter, will enable the curriculum development team to stay on course. Knowledge goals do not supplant skill and character goals; neither do they stand on their own. Together, however, knowledge, skill, and character goals constitute the training goals that guide curriculum planning.

Phase 3 – List Training Goals

Training goals identified by the curriculum development team should be listed for future reference by all participants. This list will include skill and character "outcome goals" (they do not require translation) and the knowledge goals identified in Phases 1 and 2.

It is not necessary to retain the graphic layout of the profile chart, but it is important to preserve the distinction between minimal qualifications for entrance into ministry and professional development competencies. This distinction should be reflected in knowledge as well as skill and character areas. Programme planners also will want access to the qualification priorities identified by practitioners in the profiling step. This need can be met, however, and the process simplified, by viewing the list of training goals and the profile chart as complementary documents.

When a list has been generated, it is important to assure the endorsement of each participant in the curriculum development team.

How are training goals used?

Training goals are essential to determining training responsibilities and approaches. Because outcome goals afford an incomplete picture of the training task, the curriculum development team must develop training goals before proceeding to consider training approaches or distribution of training responsibilities. Only by working from a cooperatively negotiated and endorsed list of training goals can trainers assure the coordination of training efforts.

Training goals also form the basis for programme development within the various training units. Because the training task exceeds outcome goals, programme developers must have access to training goals to assure the comprehensiveness of training and the appropriate preparation of trainees. Training goals provide programme developers with a useable list of required knowledge, skills, and character qualities which they can use to design training programmes.

Determining Training Responsibilities and Approaches

It would be easy to assume that identifying training goals has prepared us to develop the missionary training curriculum. Before moving ahead, however, we need to address two prior questions: Who is responsible for missionary training? and, How can missionary training most effectively be pursued?

Too often in the past, these questions have not been considered. Prospective missionaries simply have been required to attend Bible school or seminary for a year or more. In other situations, missionary training centres have assumed full responsibility for preparing missionaries for cross-cultural ministry. While we thank God for the significant contribution these institutions have made, a broader view and a cooperative approach to missionary preparation are more realistic and more helpful.

The questions "Who is responsible?" and "How should training be pursued?" are complicated by their interrelationship. At times, identifying the best approach to developing a particular quality or skill will indicate to whom that training responsibility should be assigned. For other training goals, clarifying who is responsible will suggest which approach is most appropriate.

How to determine training approaches and responsibilities

At this point, the curriculum development team needs to examine each training goal and agree what approach is best suited and who will assume primary responsibility for developing the missionary candidate's qualifications in that area. The sections which follow will clarify issues bearing on these decisions.

After responsibility for developing missionary qualifications has been distributed, it is best to list each training goal, in parallel columns, under the name of the organisation which has accepted that responsibility. This assures that each participant recognises the total responsibility she or he has accepted, and it allows others to see how their training responsibilities relate to those of co-operating organisations.

Why is this list important?

This list of training goals by responsible organisations is the key to efficient curriculum planning, since it indicates both entry and completion standards. If it is assumed, for example, that missionary candidates come from local congregations and attend Bible school before entering the missionary training centre, the implications are clear. The missionary training centre should establish as its entry standard minimal qualifications identified for new missionaries in the training areas allocated to home congregations and Bible schools. Likewise, the missionary training centre curriculum should be planned to assure attainment of minimal standards in all training goals allocated to the training centre staff.

It is important to note that every cooperating organisation must support all training goals through "the hidden curriculum" (discussed below). Implicit messages communicated at any point in missionary preparation rarely can be corrected by explicit instruction. Later in this chapter we will discuss the implications of "the hidden curriculum" for the missionary training centre.

Missionary Training Is a Cooperative Venture

At least six different individuals, organisations, or institutions share responsibility for preparing the missionary for effective cross-cultural ministry.

The community of missionary training

The missionary herself or himself must accept primary responsibility for obtaining the preparation required for fruitful obedience to God's missionary call. This is not to imply that the candidate should pursue a self-determined course of preparation, apart from the counsel and support of her or his church or mission agency. Rather, we acknowledge that effective missionary service flows from a life shaped by spiritual and personal disciplines and from a heart irrevocably committed to obey the Scriptures. While others may encourage and assist, only the missionary candidate herself or himself can cultivate the disciplines and the heart-obedience required for effective cross-cultural ministry.

Critical to missionary preparation—but too often overlooked— is **the missionary's home congregation**. Christianity is not an individualistic religion. The New Testament uses several metaphors for the church. It is a building, in which believers are "living stones" (1 Pet 2:5; cf. Heb 3:6). Sometimes the church is compared to a family (Mt 12:49-50; cf. 2 Cor 6:18). Most often the church is portrayed as a body in which believers are various parts, or "members," all essential, yet each with its unique function (Rom 12:4-8; 1 Cor 12:12-27). God intends believers to be part of a local congregation, subject to its leadership and under its spiritual care. The missionary's home congregation should function as both ministry context and community of faith, nurturing the spiritual life and gifts of the candidate from the time of her or his spiritual rebirth to the time of departure for the field, and beyond.

Bible schools or seminaries provide formal instruction in the Bible, its teachings, and academic disciplines useful in Christian ministry. Most Bible schools and seminaries also provide training in spiritual disciplines and ministry skills. Such training can play an important part in preparation for missionary service.

The focus of *the missionary training centre* is much narrower than that of a Bible school or seminary. Typically, missionary training centres do not provide the breadth of instruction offered by a Bible school. On the other hand, missionary training centres do provide focused instruction in the information and skills required for effective cross-cultural life and ministry.

Often *the mission agency in the homeland* is viewed only as a sending channel, rather than as a training agency, yet almost all mission agencies provide orientation or training for their personnel. Indeed, some aspects of missionary training (such as instruction in agency policies and procedures) only can be provided by the sending agency.

Since cross-cultural ministry competence is a life-long pursuit, missionary training cannot be limited to pre-field preparation. Continuing training for professional development must be planned, however, if missionaries are to realise the highest levels of spiritual maturity and ministry competence. This on-field training should be initiated by *the mission agency on the field in partnership with the receiving church*, if a church already exists. While the receiving church should not be expected to initiate on-going training of expatriate missionaries, culturally it is better situated than expatriates ever can be to identify areas where training is needed and to provide that training.

The need for cooperation in missionary training

It should be clear that none of these organisations or institutions alone can adequately prepare a candidate for missionary service. Nevertheless, examples of cooperative planning for missionary preparation are almost nonexistent. Sometimes this results from the prideful assumption that our programme is the only resource God has for the task of missionary training. More often, however, it reflects small thinking—the inability to see missionary training in terms of God's "big picture"—and impatience with the task of recruiting other organisations and agencies into a community of concern for and commitment to missionary preparation.

We all need to face the fact that *"doing it all ourselves" is dangerous!* Candidates need the communities of faith and ministry provided by home congregations and mission agencies. They also need training offered by Bible schools and missionary training centres.

Local churches need Bible schools and missionary training centres to provide specialised preparation for cross-cultural ministry. Churches also need mission agencies to facilitate sending and placement of their missionaries overseas and to provide supervision, accountability, and support services for missionaries on the field.

Mission agencies need home congregations to nurture candidates and to support missionaries—prayerfully and financially—when they are on the field. They also need Bible schools and missionary training centres to which they can direct candidates and furloughing missionaries for needed training.

Perhaps most of all, home congregations, mission agencies, missionary training centres, and missionaries need the guidance and assistance of *the church in the receiving culture*. Only with the help of those who are at home in a society can cross-cultural missionaries come to see themselves as they are perceived. Only with insights gained from national believers can missionaries learn to communicate the gospel powerfully to the hearts of a nation.

Clearly, missionary training must be approached as a cooperative task. It is useful to review the qualifications for effective missionary service identified in the training goals and ask, "Who is best able to direct, assist, and certify this aspect of the missionary's preparation?" Or, the question may be stated, "Who should be responsible for this area of missionary training?" Before these questions finally are answered, however, we need to consider the various training approaches available.

Approaches to the Training Task

All of human teaching and learning can be sorted into three basic approaches. In this section we will review these approaches, then examine the role of two of them for missionary training.

Three approaches to training

Formal education refers to schooling. To be enrolled in formal education is to go to school. Education in schools is intentional, planned, staffed, and funded. One "attends" school; that is, to take advantage of formal education, one must go to a specified place and remain there for specified blocks of time. In addition, formal education is organised by "grade" levels; a student must complete second grade before entering third grade, etc. The curriculum of formal education is dictated by the needs and expectations of society and, at higher levels, by the interests of researchers and scholars in specific discipline fields. Success in schooling entitles one to continue to the next grade level; the ultimate reward for achievement in schooling is symbolised by a certificate or degree.

Formal education is an effective way to learn new information, to develop critical thinking skills, and to acquire other skills useful for additional schooling. For missionary training, formal education (as offered by Bible schools and seminaries) is an excellent way to learn about the Bible and its teachings.

The most common approach to education is not schooling, but **informal education**. Informal education is rarely intentional or planned, and it is never staffed or funded. Informal education usually is spontaneous, arising out of life situations. Informal education can happen in any context, at any time. For this reason, informal education always occurs along with other approaches to education, whether we are aware of it or not. Of course, it occurs in contexts which are not intentionally educational, as well. Our mother tongue, the stories and traditions of our society, cultural mores and taboos, and numerous other essential and non-essential information and skills are acquired through informal education.

Informal education is the normal—and most effective—way we acquire our values and learn to express them as relational skills. In missionary training, informal education will be important to achieving those training goals aimed at developing character qualities.

Any attempt to classify all education as either formal or informal is bound to fail. Life is not that simple. *Nonformal education* lies between these two extremes. Like formal education, nonformal education is intentional, planned, staffed, and funded. Unlike school, however, nonformal education is not organised by "grades" and does not grant degrees. Like informal education, nonformal education is practical; it addresses students' needs or interests. Because of its practical orientation, nonformal education often entails teaching by example and practice. For the same reason, it also often occurs "in the field" or uses teaching methods which simulate "field" situations. A community health class on infant care, an evening course on tailoring or motorcycle maintenance, a Red Cross course on cardiac-pulmonary resuscitation (CPR), a home Bible study, and a church-sponsored course on personal evangelism are all examples of nonformal education.

Unlike either formal or informal education, nonformal education often is directed toward bringing about specific change. People enroll in a nonformal education programme when they want to acquire information or skills which will enable them to do something new or to do better something they now find difficult. In missionary training, most cross-cultural, communication, and ministry skills will be learned best through nonformal education.

Figure 3:1 portrays the similarities and differences of formal, informal, and nonformal education in visual form.

It is useless to debate which approach is best. All three are best—for certain types of learning. As we have seen, abstract concepts and ideas are best learned in formal education. Social skills and values are best picked up through informal education, along with much of the information we use daily for life and pleasure. But nonformal education is most effective in enabling us to apply new information to practical situations.

Formal education (often in Bible schools and seminaries) and informal education (in home congregations and through mission agencies) contribute significantly to missionary preparation. The

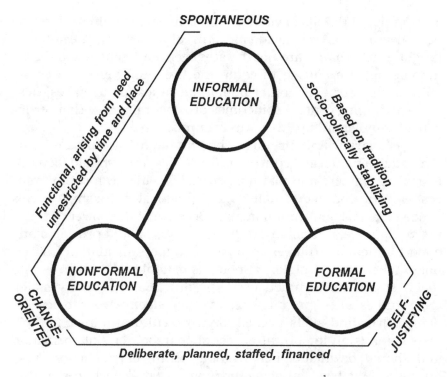

Figure 3:1. Approaches to Education[1]

missionary training centre, however, affords a unique combination of nonformal and informal preparation for missionary service.

Nonformal Education in the Missionary Training Centre

Reasons for viewing missionary training as an example of nonformal education seem like a list of comparisons between missionary training centres and Bible schools. Missionary training centres admit trainees on the basis of missionary calling and gifts, rather than on strict academic qualifications. Missionary training centres also do not offer a general education course—or even a general Bible training course—but provide a focused programme of missionary training. Each subject taught in the training centre is scheduled only as long as needed to communicate the principles

---

1. Adapted from Ward 1982:11.

and develop the skills in view; most missionary training centres do not follow a calendar of academic terms or semesters. The subjects taught, furthermore, are not dictated by tradition or social expectations, but are chosen to equip the trainee for effective cross-cultural ministry. Like other nonformal education agencies, missionary training centres sometimes provide trainees with a certificate of completion, but they rarely grant degrees.

Missionary training centres should take full advantage of the strengths of nonformal education. To do this, they should focus on recruiting trainers and planning curricula which will equip trainees with the character qualities and practical skill competencies needed for cross-cultural ministry. Because of the power of training by example, missionary training centres should provide many opportunities for trainees to observe trainers in ministry situations. Whenever possible, trainers also should take trainees into "field" situations to practise cross-cultural and ministry skills. Case studies and simulations afford other effective ways to develop perspectives and skills needed for cross-cultural ministry. Bible instruction is an important aspect of character or skill formation and should be included in training centre curricula for these purposes. Whatever other methods are used, reflection and dialogue can assure that learning occurs.

Despite the differences between Bible schools and missionary training centres, we often observe attempts to combine both in one institution. A Bible school may offer a missionary training course, or a missionary training centre may expand its curriculum to offer a full list of Bible school courses. Although it appears economical to support one educational institution instead of two, combining a Bible school and a missionary training centre is difficult, at best. The differences in admission criteria, curricular scope and focus, and training motivation and methods mean that combining Bible school and missionary training results in many stresses and tensions. Almost always one set of priorities suffers as the other succeeds.

Other, even more fundamental problems occur when we attempt to combine a Bible school and missionary training centre. Missionary training classes often are smaller than more general Bible school classes. Developing spiritual gifts and ministry skills also requires more missionary trainers than the number of lecturers needed for Bible school instruction. For these reasons, non-formal missionary training programmes often are more expensive (per trainee) than formal Bible school programmes. When funds are short and budgets must be cut, a combined Bible school and missionary training centre will find it easy to conclude that missionary training is more expensive than it can afford.

There is also the matter of prestige. Formal education programmes thrive on prestige. (Note their emphasis on "standards," "degrees," and "accreditation.") Nonformal education programmes, on the other hand, value practical training. Again, missionary training is likely to be disadvantaged by the conflicting values of these two approaches to education whenever an institution attempts to be both a Bible school and a missionary training centre.

By this we do not intend to imply that Bible schools cannot contribute to missionary education or that missionary training centres cannot provide significant Bible teaching. Rather, we should recognise that missionary candidates who study missions in a Bible school still need the practical training offered by missionary training centres. Although all missionary training centres teach the Bible, most missionary candidates should complete a basic Bible school course before entering missionary training. Bible schools and missionary training centres need to view their training programmes as complementary, not as competitive. For the reasons mentioned above, missionary training centres which attempt to offer a formal Bible school programme may jeopardise their primary training mission.

Informal Education
in the Missionary Training Centre

Because we often are unaware of informal education when it occurs, it sometimes is called "the hidden curriculum." The hidden curriculum includes all the things a trainee learns through the total experience of his or her life during the training programme, especially outside the classroom. It is the way the environment, the personalities of teachers and fellow-students, the institution's ethos, and many other nebulous but powerful factors affect perceptions and attitudes.

Although missionary trainers may have little control over some aspects of the informal curriculum, there are many things they can purposely build into the environment to affect trainees positively. It is important for the trainees to be aware of the values which have shaped the training environment, so they won't resent it as an arbitrary imposition. Three important areas of the informal curriculum are staff, facilities, and use of time.

Staff

Jesus said, "It is enough for the student to be like his teacher" (Mt 10:25) and, "Everyone who is fully trained will be like his teacher" (Lk 6:40). Who the staff are—their zeal, love, and commitment to the cause of Christ in missions—is at least as important as their knowledge of the subjects they teach or the efficiency of their administration. We must model what we want to produce. If we want scholars, let all the teachers be engrossed in scholarship. If we want missiologists, let us have missiologists as teachers. If we want missionaries, let us have staff with a zeal for hands-on missions and on-going experience. (Is this why the young evangelist enters the seminary ambitious to win the lost and leaves it ambitious to get a Ph.D.?)

This is not to imply that someone cannot be both a missiologist and a missionary. That combination in a mentor of missionaries-in-the-making is ideal but not common. The first qualification of a trainer of missionaries is to be a model of what the students are supposed to become. Trainers should evidence as many of the missionary characteristics as possible, and they should be engaged in on-going mission-related ministry in addition to working in the training programme.

Where can we get staff like that? The best missionaries seldom want to leave their fields to come and work in the training programme. Most training programmes want to train missionaries who can endure hardness and times of trial and even deprivation. The training programme often does not have the resources to pay good salaries. Because they have academic qualifications, teachers may feel entitled to remuneration commensurate with their training. Both modelling and economics may preclude their use in the missionary training centre.

Many training programmes offer their courses on a modular basis. This means a teacher can come in for a week or two to teach only his or her subject. This may fit into the schedule of a missionary who can take a short break from her field, or a furloughing missionary who cannot be tied down for a whole session.

Sometimes for family or health reasons, a missionary cannot return to the field. Such people are often recruited for missionary training. The Lord also may call active missionaries to take time out to train others. Training proceeds best when the mission agency or agencies using the training assign missionary short-term and long-term staff to work in the training programme.

If we cannot get full-time trainers or administrative staff with extensive missionary experience, we can require prospective staff to go through our training or a programme with a philosophy like our own. Part of that training should include field experience.

It is important for all staff, both administrative and teaching, to participate with students in outreaches, field trips, visits during internship, prayer, and field research. Constant staff contact with the mission field is vital if teaching and curriculum are to be kept relevant. When staff express intense interest in field ministries, trainees are encouraged to have the same attitude and to understand the significance of their own work.

The staff should include both men and women, and when possible should come from various cultural backgrounds. They should be supported in a way similar to the way the missionary trainees will be supported. The ratio of trainees to trainers needs to be low for effective modelling and mentoring. Some programmes try to have at least one staff member per four or five trainees.

There also should be planned, on-going training and vision-building activities for staff. Even good teachers benefit from learning more about foundational principles and innovative methods in training and cross-cultural ministry.

In a new training programme, there is every opportunity to set policies related to staff qualifications, recruitment, support, and training. We need to think about the informal curriculum effects as we establish personnel policies and develop our staff.

Facilities

The physical surroundings of the trainees as they learn shapes their experience. Is your programme going to be residential? By correspondence? TEE style? Will it be long term (many months or a year or more) or short term (days or weeks)? The type of programme affects the kind of facilities needed. For example, for TEE you need transportation for the trainers, and for a long-term residential programme you need a campus.

Keeping the students in their field environment allows maximum immediate application of what is learned. Long-term living in community in a residential training programme allows for closer mentoring. It brings to light spiritual and personality problems that need to be resolved. A combination of both is probably ideal.

A missions training centre can be the catalyst for both types of training. It can contain resource materials (i.e., a library), be a base for correspondence or TEE programmes, host residential training experiences of various lengths, produce and distribute textbooks and training materials, and provide on-going training of trainers.

Should a *residential site*, whether for long or short-term stays, be in a rural, isolated place or in an urban centre? Many training opportunities and discipline issues are different in the two environments. For example, "bush living" skills can be developed in the rural campus, and there are fewer off-campus distractions. It may be harder, however, to get visiting trainers to come to a rural location. In the city, students may be distracted by bits of shopping or visiting friends, so that they frequently miss parts of the daily training schedule. On the other hand, many training resources, both materials and people, are more accessible in the city. There is more opportunity to practise urban mission skills, and there are more local churches with which students can be involved. We need to choose, depending on what we are trying to accomplish.

What kind of *living accommodations* should be provided? Do we want something similar to what students will face on the mission field, something similar to what they are used to at home, or something else? What will best meet our purposes? In-service trainees who are coming from the hardships of a remote field may need the relief of more comfortable housing than new recruits who need to be hardened for the field. We also need to decide if staff housing should be of a different standard from student housing.

Housing policies will affect a trainee's experience. Does the administration place students of various ethnic or denominational backgrounds in the same room so that there will be forced interaction? How will conflicts that arise be handled? Is the accommodation suitable for families or only for singles? Who will supervise housekeeping duties and child care?

Then there is the issue of *food*. Will the students eat communally? For every meal? Who will cook, and whose type of food will be prepared (if the school is inter-cultural)? Will staff share in the communal eating? Will families with small children be able to participate? Should the students each cook for themselves and be encouraged to share with each other, since this is what they will likely have to do on the field? How can we encourage an interest in eating the food of other cultures?

And then, what *equipment* will the programme need? Are there vehicles, typewriters, desks, classrooms, computers, projectors, duplicating machines, cooking pots, textbooks, libraries, cassette recorders, and video equipment that need to be acquired? Should we teach people to use equipment they normally will not have in their own ministries? Can we teach them less technical methods of doing the same thing? Can they learn to use advanced technology, as well as how to avoid becoming dependent on it?

Again, all these decisions should be made with an eye on what we are indirectly saying to the trainees by how things are run. It is true that "the medium is the message." We always must ask ourselves, "What ministry and training commitments does this arrangement convey?"

Use of Time

The daily, weekly, and yearly schedules show our priorities in the way we use time. They shape our experience.

It is through the time given to *scheduled activities* that much of the spiritual formation is done. Many residential training programmes schedule communal prayer and worship very early each morning, in addition to time allocated to personal devotions. Some set aside a period of fasting and prayer each week and all-night prayer each month. Other prayer, Bible teaching, worship, exhortation, counselling, and fellowship activities come up regularly in the schedule to encourage development of spiritual life and interpersonal skills. Habits of regular spiritual exercises will be needed on the mission field if the new missionaries want to keep close to the Lord. The amount of time given to these activities and the zeal of staff in attending and supporting them convey to the students their importance. These activities are a big part of our curriculum, so students should not feel free to skip them any more than to skip classes.

If the competencies include knowing how to unwind and pace work, recreational activities will be part of the schedule, as well. Campus clean-up gives time to develop housekeeping skills and a servant spirit. Training outside the centre also may be part of the schedule, such as regular times for witnessing or other ministry.

The *class schedule* depends a lot on the available teachers. Many training programmes rely on part-time, volunteer teachers. Often the teachers are more available if you can schedule their entire course as a module of a week or two. It usually is wise for the programme staff to have some modules or activities on hand in case visiting teachers do not show up when expected. This models flexibility and good use of time.

The *yearly schedule*, with the amount of time given to residential learning and to field work, says much about our philosophy of training. We need a balance that best allows us to cover the competencies we are trying to produce. The times of the year for class work and field work also must be considered. Is it farming season? Will target peoples in the field have time to listen to preachers? Do the trainees themselves need time off to farm? Are roads passable at this time of year? You can think of other such considerations in your own area.

A Word of Caution

Divergent cultural backgrounds can influence the effects of "the hidden curriculum" in unexpected ways. This is especially true if most of those planning the training programme are not of the same cultural background as the trainees. The planners might make decisions regarding informal curricular issues, not realising that the effect on missionary trainees may be very different from that expected. For example, a person from one culture might think that having trainers live in the dormitory with trainees will give the trainer more credibility, while in actual fact, in the trainees' culture, it will give less. Plenty of consultation with people of various backgrounds might be needed before the most useful arrangements are made. There should also be evaluations afterward, when trainees have an opportunity to comment on how effective the programme was in their own lives.

Conclusion

This chapter has provided guidance for programme developers in three areas. First, instructions were given for identifying knowledge goals. Second, advice was provided for distributing training responsibilities, with consideration given to training approaches. And third, a framework for distributing responsibilities was set by identifying the training community and by describing and illustrating training approaches.

The product of this process is a list of training goals, with primary responsibility for achieving each goal allocated to—and accepted by—one member of the training community. With this list, trainers can return to their own organisations—i.e., their churches, mission agencies, Bible schools, or the missionary training centre—and plan training programmes. Furthermore, they can be confident the programmes they plan will integrate smoothly with those of other training units and that missionary trainees will be sent to the field with the knowledge, skills, and character qualities required for effective missionary service.

It is this process of institution-based programme planning—planning specific programmes and lessons—to which we now must turn our attention.

Chapter 4

Writing Learning Objectives

Stephen Hoke

Rev. Owandere had been a missionary for twelve years in West Africa, and he was thrilled with the invitation to help train the next generation of missionaries going out from his country. But as he sat in the shade planning his "Introduction to Missions" course, he grew increasingly anxious. He had so much he wanted to say, and so little time. He had experienced so much, and he wondered how best to put his experiences into communicable form. He wanted to share his heart with these young candidates, but he couldn't see a way to organise all he had learned and experienced into a coherent *course plan.*

Half the globe away in Manila, Rosa Macagba grappled with the same frustration in planning a lesson at the newly established missionary training centre. After two terms among an unreached people group in Southeast Asia, she was asked by her mission to become a lecturer and mentor for missionary interns. She could clearly visualise the ideal missionary needed, and she had stacks of notes and ideas she wanted to mold into courses and presentations. But how to shape her first *lesson*? How could she be sure that what she wanted to say would actually be helpful in moving the candidates toward the established goals? How should she focus her thoughts into a process that would be educationally effective?

These two trainers are facing a typical problem—how to transform their commitments and goals into a training plan, into

65

curriculum. In this chapter we will outline a step-by-step process for trainers to translate their ideas into learning objectives. Chapter 5 will help you turn these objectives into meaningful learning experiences. Whether you are working at the macro-level in planning *courses* or at the micro-level in planning particular *lessons* within a longer course, the principles you apply in the process are the same.

Chapter Objectives: This chapter is designed to help you—

- define learning objectives and their role in missionary training
- write clear learning objectives for missionary training following the model suggested

Defining Learning Objectives and Their Role in Missionary Training

Defining Curriculum

To begin, it may be helpful to clarify how we use the word *curriculum.* The word literally means a pre-determined path along which a race is run, a "racecourse." Traditionally, the curriculum was considered the *content* that a student was expected to master before moving on. More recently, the term connotes the *activity of the student* as she moves through a variety of experiences which involve content, skills, and character issues (LeBar and Plueddemann 1989:254). We are using an even broader definition which reflects our assumptions and values.

Various definitions and approaches to curriculum development have been suggested which reflect distinctive value orientations and commitments in the field. Consider the following:

1. Curriculum is the content that is made available to the students.

2. Curriculum is the planned and guided learning experiences of students.

3. Curriculum is the actual experiences of a student or participant.

4. Generally, curriculum includes both the materials and the experiences for learning. Specifically, curriculum is the written courses for study used for Christian education.

5. Curriculum is the organisation of learning activities guided by a teacher with the intent of changing behaviour.[1]

6. Curriculum is the interface between intentions and operations—between the why and the what/how of an educational activity (Ward 1979:1).

7. Curriculum is the entire set of processes used to identify learner needs and cooperate with the learner in meeting those needs (McKean 1977:1).

We will use the word "curriculum" in its broadest sense, that is, the entire learning environment in which intentional learning takes place. Any time we decide what others should do in order to enable them to become or to do something else, we are planning curriculum. Here are some examples of curriculum:

- A missionary and his twenty-two-year-old disciple are having lunch together. They talk about work, family, and pressures of the day. They read the Bible and pray. The missionary embraces the young man before he has to hurry off to catch the bus back to work.
- Later, the missionary's wife reads a bed-time Bible story to two preschool children. They talk about Jesus stilling the storm. The mother listens to the children's fears about bad dreams and talks about Jesus' care all through the night.

These are planned activities that seek to bring both the new convert and the missionaries' children a step nearer to maturity in Christ. Curriculum includes the setting or context in which the learning takes place—whether inside or outside, whether a home or the workplace; the content that is made available to students; and the actual learning experiences guided by a trainer, mentor, or helper.

Shared Responsibility

This definition of curriculum implies that the trainer and the trainee share responsibility for the learning process. The trainer assumes responsibility for planning and implementing content and experiences, while the trainee assumes responsibility for

---

1. Definitions 1-5 are from Pazmino (1987:31).

actively and intentionally participating in the learning process (LeBar and Plueddemann 1989:280).

Another helpful way to understand curriculum is as "the educational planning that leads to the actual teaching experience" (Plueddemann 1987:56-57). Essentially, a curriculum is an educational plan. It is a road map for how to get where you want to go and what you will do to get there. Plueddemann suggests that the curriculum plan includes three major components: the assumed teaching-learning context, the intended outcomes in the life of the student (what we are calling the "profile"), and the intended educational activities. To determine the effectiveness of missionary training, therefore, it is not enough only to evaluate learning outcomes; we also must evaluate the educational activities, including the appropriateness of intended outcomes and learning activities in the teaching-learning context. (See Chapter 6 for a procedure which applies this insight.)

Training as Science and Art

Training is a science, an art, and a gift. As a science, effective training is based on principles that emerge from research that can be learned by study and enhanced by skillful implementation. Educators tend to talk about this aspect of training quite a lot, because the "science" of training can be taught.

As an art, training calls for relational sensitivity, intuition, flexibility in uncertainty, and timing. These artistic people-skills are largely natural talents but can be developed by training and practice. Donald Schon (1983) suggests that the skill of an effective teacher-artist depends on putting what one knows into action in day-to-day practice. The art is finely tuned by consciously thinking about (reflecting on) what one is doing, often while doing it. "Stimulated by surprise, [effective teachers] turn thought back on action and on the learning which is implicit in action." As a teacher-trainer tries to make sense of what is happening in the midst of the teaching-learning process, he or she "also reflects on the understandings which have been implicit in his action, understandings which he surfaces, criticises, restructures, and includes in further action." Schon concludes: "It is this entire process of reflection-in-action which is central to the 'art' by which practitioners sometimes deal well with situations of uncertainty, instability, uniqueness, and value conflict" (Schon 1983:50).

In addition, the Apostle Paul names teaching as one of the equipping spiritual gifts (Eph 4:11-12; Rom 12:7; 1 Cor 12:28). Teaching involves a special spiritual empowerment or enabling by the Holy Spirit to equip or train Christians toward maturity in Jesus Christ or effectiveness in ministry. Science can be taught, art can be developed, but a gift only can be exercised.

The Flow of Curriculum Planning

A cascading waterfall provides a useful image to visualise the process of curriculum planning (see Figure 4:1). Although not all educational plans proceed so neatly in such a linear fashion, the analogy is helpful in illustrating the relationship of the component elements in the process.

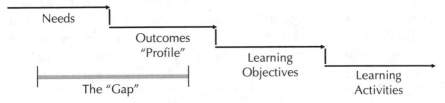

Figure 4:1. The Downward Cascade

Since learning starts where the trainee is, then course and lesson planning must begin with the needs of the trainees. What do they already know? What skills have they developed? What skills and character traits do they possess? This is the starting or entry point of the learning process. Determining *entry level* characteristics in understanding (knowledge), skills, and character is one way to control the level at which courses will be taught. This can be done by setting entry qualifications or requirements, by measuring incoming trainees and adapting training to their needs, or by a combination of both. When entry qualifications are set, incoming students that meet all requirements should be able to move into training without difficulty. Students who do not meet entry requirements, however, may require special tutoring to acquire basic understandings and skills, as well as individualised mentoring to address character deficiencies. Brian Massey's case study (see Figure 4:2) suggests another creative way to measure incoming trainees vis-à-vis the training goal.

The next stage in the progressive planning flow is to compare the trainees' entry level characteristics with the outcomes profile (see Chapter 2). When you measure the trainees against the outcomes profile, you identify a "gap" between where they are now and where they need to be upon completion of training.

Stating clear learning objectives in terms of the "gap" is the third stage. Learning objectives are tools which break the larger, more comprehensive learning goals into smaller, more attainable steps. Learning objectives flow from the profile and point the way in which the trainee will grow.

Finally, appropriate learning activities are designed to "close the gap." Learning activities help bridge the gap between the trainee's present status and the desired goal. They are *strategies for accomplishing* the instructional objectives. Learning activities should flow naturally from the needs, outcomes, and learning objectives you have identified. They answer the question, *What kinds of experiences do we need to provide to help trainees become who they need to be and to do what they need to be able to do?*

The Australia/New Zealand Experiment

A working group of nine missionary trainers representing eight organisations met in Australia and New Zealand in mid-1994 to develop an inter-mission Pre-Departure Orientation (PDO) pro-gramme. Their profiling exercise led them to an issue not addressed in the Pasadena seminar—how to adequately assess the participant on entry to an existing training course. They recognised that the "gap" between the entry point and exit point defines what needs to be taught, but how the entry and end points are determined needed to be designed.

They borrowed the idea of a "Competency Continuum" from the training department of a leading manufacturer. This continuum had been designed to provide attainment levels within each competency for workers. Examples of low, mid, and high levels are given on a

---

Figure 4:2

continuum, and each person is able to assess his or her current level and plot it appropriately. PDO participants arrive having plotted on each of the continuum lines their assessment of their level of competency. This exercise builds a profile of each participant *on entry* to the programme. The participant, together with the course coordinator, uses this self-assessment to develop a set of learning objectives for the course. These are recorded on a learning contract. When the course is complete, the personal learning objectives are reviewed, and competencies are replotted along the continuum, again by self-assessment. The result is a profile of the participant *on exit*. The following three examples illustrate the PDO competency assessment levels:

Adaptation:	Low	Mid	High
Identification:	Low	Mid	High
Communication:	Low	Mid	High

Several guidelines should be noted. First, the competency continuum levels, especially at the high end, are not expected to be achieved solely as a result of the course. Many will only be developed through cross-cultural living experience, and therefore the continuum will be of assistance to the missionary as a personal review aid.

Second, it is possible that participants may discover that their initial assessment of a competency level was too high, and therefore on exit they actually see themselves as less competent. But that is OK; that is what is needed—a realistic understanding of where they are now. The course will have given them growth skills to enable them to develop in that area, along with all the others.

Third, this concept is firmly based on the principles of both Adult Education and Competency-Based Education—the learner is the focus and is responsible for the learning. Hence the decision to allow the participants to set their own learning objectives, rather than set them ourselves for the course curriculum elements.

Source: Massey 1994

Figure 4:2 (cont.)

The waterfall image also illustrates the natural flow from the general content of a course to the specific content of a particular lesson (see Figure 4:3). A *course* (sometimes called a *subject*) in "Missionary Life," for example, might include *units* on Bible study, Christian character, culture adaptation, and cross-cultural communication. These units, in turn, will be broken down into *lessons* on such topics as Developing Holy Habits, Living the Spirit-Filled Life, Coping with Culture Shock, and Following Jesus' Model of Communication. Notice how a particular *lesson* cascades naturally from one or several *units*, which flow out of the selected *course* content. The flow should be logical, natural, and interrelated, not forced or disconnected.

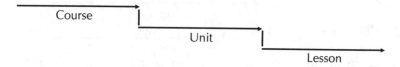

Figure 4:3. The Natural (Logical) Integration of Content

Balanced Learning

We are committed to balanced learning that includes knowledge (*understanding*), being (*character qualities*), and doing (*ministry skills*) (see Figure 4:4). Whenever we talk about writing objectives, our intention is objectives that promote learning in all three dimensions, although certain activities and experiences may focus on only one or two dimensions at a time.

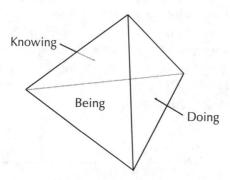

Figure 4:4. The Three Dimensions of Balanced Learning

The first dimension, *understanding*, often can be demonstrated by explaining or describing a truth. *Ministry skill* can usually be demonstrated by doing a particular activity, such as preaching, witnessing, building, or planning. It may be helpful to remember, however, that the third dimension, *being*, often is not best measured by behaviour or action. Inner *character qualities* are more subtle, intangible, and therefore more difficult to quantify or measure. *Values* and *feelings* also are more difficult to demonstrate and measure. That doesn't mean we can't evaluate progress in the area of character formation, but it does mean that we must exercise care and discernment in writing objectives that are appropriate for that dimension of missionary growth.

A balanced view of learning prevents curriculum planners and trainers from placing too much emphasis on mere information and knowledge gained in an academic setting, apart from the being and doing dimensions. Growth and development biblically understood keep knowing and obedience inseparably linked. Truth is "known" only when it is obeyed.

The Place of Objectives in Teaching and Learning

Setting objectives is a necessary step in developing a missionary training curriculum. "If you aim at nothing, you will be sure to hit it" is a self-evident truth. Unfortunately, setting objectives is a step often omitted by trainers. As you look at the primary learning needs of your trainees, you should begin to develop specific objectives to meet those needs. Some needs or learning tasks may require more than one objective in order to have that need adequately met. In other cases, perhaps one objective will meet several needs.

Writing objectives can be understood as defining the specific learning steps to bridge the "gap" between what is and what is not yet. The statement of an objective answers the question, *What does the trainee need to be able to **understand** (know), to **be** (character qualifications), or to **do** (behaviour or ministry skill)? How can the trainee demonstrate that he or she has achieved the learning goals?* Objectives describe a desired state in the trainee.

A meaningfully stated objective is one that succeeds in communicating the trainer's intent to the trainee. That implies that the trainee shares responsibility with the trainer for the learning process. It is not enough for the trainer to state clearly his or her purposes for a course or lesson, then proceed as if successful learning depends only on the skill of the trainer. The trainee must respond to the trainer's stated intent and must actively participate in the activities in order for an objective to be realised.

Before we proceed to specific instructions for writing objectives, a word of caution is in order. Some efforts at writing objectives may be unsatisfactory because the goals which are sought cannot be reduced to behavioural terms. It is dangerous to assume (as some educators teach) that only observable behaviours or qualities evidenced through behaviours are real. In Scripture we see a number of commands that are not stated in behavioural terms. For example, the Great Commandment in Matthew 22:37, "Love the Lord your God with all your heart and with all your soul and with all your mind," is not behavioural. While Jesus' words to his disciples, "If you love me, you will obey what I command" (Jn 14:15), seems to be behavioural, yet we know that commandment-keeping does not always indicate genuine love (note the Pharisees!).

Another mistake is to assume that stating a desirable outcome in behavioural terms makes it a helpful objective. Sometimes a "means-end" shift occurs that is totally counter-productive. Suppose a trainer, in a course on "The Missionary's Prayer Life," set a goal to enlarge the role of prayer in the life of her trainees. That certainly is a worthy goal. Yet notice what happens if we announce the behavioural objective, "By the fourth week of the course, the trainee will pray sixty minutes each day." Praying sixty minutes a day, which was intended to deepen communication with God, easily can shift to become an *end* in itself. The number of minutes trainees "pray" can become the goal! For those who believe God is more concerned with the heart than with outward behaviour, this is a fatal shift.

Ted Ward (1994) suggests that instructional objectives are most helpful for the lower levels of cognitive learning (e.g., recognition, recall, and comprehension), but they are not as helpful, even useless, for the higher levels of thinking (e.g., evaluation, application, and synthesis). You will discover that you cannot write specific objectives for every value, behaviour, or character trait that you want people to develop.[2]

To the extent that writing learning objectives helps you identify the understanding, skill, or quality that you wish trainees to develop, use learning objectives to guide your lesson planning. Remember, though, that there are understandings that are difficult to quantify, skills which cannot be measured or observed easily, and character qualities that defy definition in behavioural form. When you encounter these issues, state "faith goals" (Plueddemann 1994) rather than behavioural objectives.

Finally, writing objectives is a dynamic and developmental activity. It requires changes, additions, and refinements as the trainer interacts with trainees—their uniqueness and growth—and with change in the training or ministry context. I often have regarded objectives I have written with great pride, only to realise two weeks into my course that my objectives were incomplete, that the verbs I selected no longer seem accurate, or that the students actually need to spend time on different qualities or skills than I had anticipated. This situation forces me to rewrite some objectives and to draft entirely new ones I had missed.

Writing Objectives That Communicate

The most helpful teaching-learning objectives adhere to specific standards (Goad 1982:65; cf. Benson 1993):

1. There is no doubt on the part of the trainee about what is required.

2. Action is the trainee's, not the trainer's or anyone else's.

3. Performance is unambiguous. After an attempt is made, it is possible for the trainee or the trainer to tell clearly whether the objective has been achieved. (This is easiest when the performance can be measured in some meaningful way.)

---

2. Kemp (1977:34-38) highlights the difficulty in specifying objectives in the affective area—attitudes, values, and appreciations—in clearly observable and measurable terms. Realistically, there are many important training goals that cannot be reduced to measurable objectives. Eisner (1969:13-18), a critic of behavioural objectives, suggests the term "expressive objectives" for those specific outcomes which cannot be stated readily in behavioural terms.

4. Clear, precise, action words are used (whenever possible and when appropriate).

There are three essential ingredients to writing clear objectives. The first is the *performance* or *behaviour*—what you want the trainee to be able to do. The second is the *condition* under which the performance is to be obtained. The third is the *standard of performance*. Let's take these steps one at a time.

Identifying Desired Behaviour

First, *identify the final performance or behaviour with a specific action word.* Unfortunately, there are many common verbs which are open to a wide range of interpretations, which mean different things to different people. Consider the following verbs in this light (Mager 1975:20):

Words Open to Many Interpretations	Words Open to Fewer Interpretations
to know	to write
to understand	to recite
to *really* understand	to identify
to appreciate	to differentiate
to *fully* appreciate	to solve
to enjoy	to list
to believe	to compare
to have faith in	to contrast

Why do the words on the left lead to discussions and debate regarding their meaning and application? It is because they require judgment, rather than simple observation. Whenever behavioural objectives are appropriate, it is helpful to ask, *Did I describe what the trainee will do (action word!) to show that he or she has acquired the knowledge, has mastered the skills, or evidences the character qualities which are needed?* Thus the statement that communicates best will be one that describes—at least clearly enough to avoid misinterpretation—a *behaviour* which indicates the intended learning.

Evaluate the following example objectives. Which is more helpful in determining whether a candidate actually values the importance of language learning?

Objectives Regarding Language Learning

A. To develop an understanding of the importance of language learning.

B. When the trainee completes the training module, he/she must be able to state three reasons language learning is vital to effective missionary work.

Figure 4:5

Note that the word "understanding" is open to many different meanings, is difficult to measure, and doesn't indicate exactly what you want the trainee to be able to do after a course in language learning. The second objective (B) is accomplished only when the trainee can explain *why* language learning is vital to missionaries. The ability to *explain* a concept to others not only requires that a person comprehend the main ideas, but also assumes the ability to state the reasons that language learning is important. Thus, "to state" is a more helpful verb because it identifies more precisely what you want the trainee to be able to do.

There is no doubt about what is expected when objectives are complete and precise. The key is to use *action* words, denoting something that can be measured and/or observed. It is easy to see that "understanding" is extremely difficult to measure. The words "state," "show," and "solve," on the other hand, are precise and measurable.

Which of the following objectives has identified the *end result* most specifically?

Objectives Identifying the End Result

A. The trainee will learn the Bible verses presented in this lesson.

B. The trainee will memorise the Bible verses presented in this lesson.

C. The trainee will love the Bible verses presented in this lesson.

Figure 4:6

Note that the word "learn" is somewhat ambiguous—does it mean "memorise" (as in B)? or "state the meaning of"? or "obey"? "Loving" God's Word certainly is the highest goal, and it is not ambiguous, but it is manifested in many different ways, and recognising love does demand judgment. The most specific objective, therefore, is "to memorise."

Try your hand at writing a few objectives. How would you want a candidate to demonstrate the following?

Character Quality	Possible Objective
Acceptance	
Endurance	
Forgiveness	
Joy	
Patience	

Describing Conditions for Behaviour

The second element of a learning objective is a statement of the conditions for behaviour. After identifying the desired behaviour, try to define that behaviour further by *describing the important conditions* under which the behaviour will be expected to occur. Be detailed enough to assure that the behaviour will be recognised by another competent person and that it will not be mistaken as indicating understandings, skills, or character qualities other than those intended. Conditions may specify time, place, participants, or other aspects of the expected situation. Note how the condition is illustrated in Figure 4:5, Objective B, above:

Condition: When the trainee completes the training module...

Performance: ...state three reasons language learning is vital

Now evaluate the following objectives. Which is more helpful in describing the conditions under which the behaviour will be expected to occur?

Objectives Regarding Interpersonal Conflict

A. The trainee will be able to resolve interpersonal conflicts on the mission field.

B. Given a typical interpersonal conflict situation occurring on the mission field, the trainee will be able to describe at least two different but culturally appropriate ways to resolve the conflict.

Figure 4:7

By providing a specific case in which the trainee is to resolve an interpersonal conflict, the second objective narrows the broad area of interpersonal conflict resolution to a manageable task.

Performance: ...the trainee will be able to describe at least two different but culturally appropriate ways to resolve the conflict.

Condition: Given a typical interpersonal conflict situation occurring on the mission field...

See if you can detect which of the following three objectives describes the important *conditions* most specifically:

Objectives Describing Conditions of Behaviour

A. Given an encounter with a non-Christian Pokot woman in northwest Kenya, the trainee will pray powerfully.

B. When anxious, the trainee will pray powerfully.

C. When under direct spiritual attack, the trainee will pray powerfully.

Figure 4:8

Specifying the Standard

The third step in writing clear learning objectives is to specify the standard of acceptable performance. This is done by describing how well the trainee must perform to be acceptable. Examples of how standards may be stated include the following:

- an accuracy of 80%
- according to the plans provided
- [listing] at least five characteristics for each
- in a culturally appropriate way
- in keeping with biblical principles

Which of the following objectives is more helpful in describing the conditions under which the behaviour will be expected to occur?

Objectives Regarding Language Acquisition

A. The trainee will speak Japanese fluently.

B. After nine months of language study, the trainee will be able to converse at an intermediate level with a native Japanese speaker on topics of home and community life.

Figure 4:9

This example helps us see that it sometimes is necessary to specify several conditions for demonstrating learning, but we also see the usefulness of clearly stated standards. Consider this analysis of Figure 4:9, Objective B:

Performance:	the trainee will be able to converse
Conditions:	After nine months of language study,....
	[converse] with a native Japanese speaker
	[converse] on topics of home and community life
Standard:	[converse] at an intermediate level

Stating the standard in each learning objective you write is not absolutely necessary. Whenever it makes sense to do so, however, and whenever it helps you specify the kind of performance you want, try to indicate a meaningful standard.

See if you can detect which objective specifies the *standard* or *criterion* most clearly:

Objectives Specifying the Standard of Performance

A. Upon completion of this course, the trainee will effectively experience a deepened prayer life.

B. Upon completion of this course, the trainee will experience a deepened prayer life, as assessed by the trainer.

C. Upon completion of this course, the trainee will experience a deepened prayer life, evidenced in a growing love for God, an expanding desire to pray, and increasing power in intercession.

Figure 4:10

Did you observe that all three of the objectives stated in this box include standards of performance? In A, however, "effectively" affords little guidance for either trainer or trainee to assess the learning that was achieved. Objective B affirms the right and responsibility of the trainer to judge the trainee's development. At times this may be appropriate—even necessary—but it is of little help to the trainee. The specific standards included in Objective C, on the other hand, may be the most helpful to trainers and trainees alike.

Finally...

The paragraphs above describe all but one of the necessary ingredients for a clearly written objective. The missing ingredient is assumed yet primary: the Holy Spirit directs and shapes your thinking in the process. To ensure the proper mix of this ingredient, bathe your assessing, thinking, and planning in prayer. Ask the Lord for discernment and direction in your writing and decision making. As he leads your thinking, you will sense that your objectives are truly Spirit-led.

Three further words of caution: First, build into your objectives some sort of accountability. *Who* will check to see if an objective has been achieved, and *how*? Who is responsible to verify that the objective has been accomplished? Is verbal evidence (oral or written) appropriate? Is simulated ministry (a role play or case study) a reliable context for assessment? Should the trainee be observed in ministry?

Second, involve as many people as possible in developing and approving the objectives. A highly participatory process could involve several trainers, former students, and even some current or future students, not just one trainer.

Third, continuing discussion of learning objectives with your trainees is vital. It will keep your trainees focused on the target. Start each instructional unit by listing the learning objectives, refer to them as you proceed through the exercises, and review the objectives as you conclude a particular module. Without continual discussion of objectives, it is easy for trainees to lose track of what you are doing or why you are doing it.

Practise what you have learned by doing Exercise 4:1, below.

Exercise 4:1
Writing Learning Objectives
for Four Competency Phases

On your own:

1. Select one or two competencies from the chart below.

2. Under each category of competencies, write two different learning objectives for at least three of the competency phases (sub-skills of the competency). See the Profile of Asian Missionary Trainers in Appendix D for a list of competency phases.

COMPETENCIES

1. Spiritual Maturity

Competency Phase 1: _____

Objective 1:

Objective 2:

Competency Phase 2: _____

Objective 1:

Objective 2:

---

1. **Spiritual Maturity (cont.)**
   Competency Phase 3: _____
   Objective 1:

   Objective 2:

2. **Family**
   Competency Phase 1: _____
   Objective 1:

   Objective 2:

   Competency Phase 2: _____
   Objective 1:

   Objective 2:

   Competency Phase 3: _____
   Objective 1:

   Objective 2:

3. **Relational Skills**
   Competency Phase 1: _____
   Objective 1:

   Objective 2:

   Competency Phase 2: _____
   Objective 1:

   Objective 2:

   Competency Phase 3: _____
   Objective 1:

   Objective 2:

3. Have you effectively focused on the *knowing* (understanding), *doing* (skills), and *being* (character qualities) dimensions you intended? If so, continue writing. If not, rework each objective until you have crafted the verb, the conditions, and the standard in each.

4. For which competencies do you need to write more specific learning objectives? Write at least one clear objective for each competency you want your trainees to develop. Then critique your own work for balance and completeness.

Chapter 5

Designing Learning Experiences

Stephen Hoke

Kweku was both excited and a little apprehensive. The first group of missionary candidates was scheduled to attend the three-week pre-field orientation session at the West Africa Training Centre, and Kweku was planning the sessions he would lead. This would be his first opportunity to train young candidates, and he was eager to plan interactive sessions that would actively engage all participants and significantly improve their self-awareness and skills. He wanted to translate into the daily schedule of experiences the objectives he had written with the training team. He wondered if he would be as effective as he hoped in combining reading, writing, discussion, exploration, prayer and worship, group work, and learning projects into a meaningful course of instruction. Kweku wanted to build on the Centre's existing curriculum, but he also intended to add some spice with new learning experiences. As he sat down in the Centre library, he bowed his head to ask the Master Teacher for wisdom and insight.

Like Kweku, many missionary trainers are faced with a task that is at once awesome and exciting. Around the world the opportunity exists for missionary training to become highly responsive to the needs of emerging missionaries, flexible to local needs and resources, and contextualised within the cultural setting in which the training is conducted. There is a need to look back and borrow from what has been done in the past, as well as to look forward and design new training models and learning experiences for the next generation of cross-cultural missionaries.

Chapter Objectives: This chapter is designed to help you—

- inventory learning exercises already available in your setting
- design learning experiences to help trainees develop the desired competencies

This chapter is written for two groups of people at two levels of experience. The first group consists of those persons with little or no previous teaching or training experience, for whom the task of creating a missionary training programme is a totally new and challenging experience. The step-by-step approach presented in this chapter is designed to make the design process as clear and simple as possible. Try using this approach, because it works. Learn the basic dynamics of designing an instructional programme, so that you will be equipped to branch out on your own the next time you engage in this activity.

The second group consists of those persons with some or a great deal of previous training experience. You may want to skim this chapter in search of new ideas to improve what you are already doing and for training tips on how to go beyond where you are now.

Overview

All the planning you have done to this point has prepared you to select your methods and design the teaching-learning activities for your instructional plan. Only after you have clarified your training commitments, set training goals, assessed the needs of your trainees, and identified clear learning objectives can you effectively design appropriate training strategies and choose the right methods. Now you must decide how to achieve your objectives in order to meet your trainees' needs.

Principles of Learning and Development

The term "learning experiences" refers to a variety of inter-actions between the trainees and the external conditions in the environment to which the trainees can respond. A learning experience might take place in a classroom or in a sanctuary, on a campus or on a field trip, alone or in a small group with other trainees.

Instructional Planning Is a Creative Process

If (as suggested in Chapter 4) the role of the educator-trainer is a mix of science, art, and gift, then developing one's repertoire of teaching-learning strategies is critical to the success of both the scientist and the artist in us. Clearly, this process includes relationship building and community building strategies, not merely plans for transferring ideas into heads or onto paper in an efficient manner.

Designing and preparing for instruction, then, is a creative process that follows certain patterns, while constantly surprising both the trainer and the trainee with the unexpected. Using the image of learners and disciples as *pilgrims*, Jim and Carol Plueddemann warn against being too rigid or predetermined in this learning process:

Precise goals are alien for pilgrims who are facing unpredictable dangers on the road. There are too many precarious experiences along the path. Pilgrims must have a strong sense of direction and destination, but they are not specifically sure where the path will lead in the near future. Leaders (and trainers) who get bogged down with measurable, short-term objectives often miss unfolding opportunities that arise around them.... We are headed to a heavenly city. We are concerned with the inner character development of pilgrims. We are fighting for the souls of people. The most important things in life and in eternity are not easily measurable: "So we fix our eyes not on what is seen, but on what is unseen. For what is seen is temporary, but what is unseen is eternal" (2 Cor 4:17) (Plueddemann and Plueddemann 1990:73-74).

The Plueddemanns' concluding caution provides a helpful balance:

Pilgrim educators who are deeply committed to promoting the development of people for the glory of God are not afraid to stumble about. But the stumbling is not random or irrational—but purposeful. We need to plan with much common sense and clearly focus on a vision. But for some reason, God intended for life to be unpredictable—at least from our perspective. Educational administrators and management experts long to be in control of results. But while God gives us a significant task, he does not allow us to be in control of our own lives or want us to control the lives of other people. And yet our stumbling is not aimless or purposeless. We stumble about led by the unseen hand of a loving Father who delights in giving us joyful surprises (Plueddeman 1991:3).

Learning Proceeds Best in Community

Learning is not primarily an individual endeavour. It is a small group experience. Living and learning together provides a setting where sustained, personal interaction can take place. This is not a "hit and run" approach. Rather, it is life-on-life exposure in familiar, non-threatening settings. The more closely missionary training centres can reproduce a family environment—a learning community—the more powerful will be the teaching-learning impact on trainees. A learning community provides for loving acceptance and trust of each member, nurtures the growth and development process, and creates frequent natural settings in which people can share needs, reflect on their experience, talk about what they are discovering, and be vulnerable in admitting what is difficult to apply to themselves and change about themselves.

Action Is Essential to Learning

Currently, training practitioners advocate using strategies related to *experiential, active,* or *discovery* learning. This means that trainees participate in activities—such as role play, discussion, hands-on practice—that help them discover how to be effective in ministry. In contrast, *didactic* strategies involve telling or showing trainees what to do. Learning takes place through the active participation of *trainees*—not essentially or necessarily through activities of the trainer. (Note the comparative retention rates in Figure 5:1.) That is not to say the trainer's role is unimportant. The trainer's most fundamental influence, however, is in designing an environment to stimulate and encourage learning.

Instructional Method	Recall 3 Hours Later	Recall 3 Days Later
Listening alone ("telling")	70%	10%
Looking alone ("showing")	72%	20%
Listening and looking ("show and tell")	85%	65%

Figure 5:1. Recall Rates of Three Instructional Methods
(Detonni 1993:110)

The key to effective instruction is *active participation of trainees*. Participatory strategies in which students take an active role in listening, looking, and doing instructional activities contribute to a more "holistic" learning experience, in which various senses are employed and both the logical/analytic and sensory/artistic sides of the brain are used.

Reflection Enables Learning to Be Developmental

Effective missionary training will best be done in learning communities characterised by love, acceptance, and trust. It will feature dialogue and reflection on present realities and missionary methods in light of biblical truth and the Great Commission (Groome 1980:184-195). This critical reflection, which is so vital to adult learning, draws upon three skills: (1) *critical reason* to evaluate the present (observe the obvious and probe beneath the surface to causes and meanings); (2) *critical memory* to uncover patterns and principles from the past so as to break open new understanding in the present; and (3) *critical imagination* to envision what God desires for all peoples in the future (Groome 1980:185-187). Thus, adult, nonformal, professional training should emphasise principled instruction and reflection, modelling and reflection, case studies and reflection, field trips and reflection, simulated ministry experiences and reflection, immersion experiences and reflection, journalling and dialogue reflection, etc.

An Instructional Planning Sequence[1]

Planning instruction comes easily to some trainers and much more slowly and laboriously to others. We have observed that teaching is a science, an art, and a gift. To some, planning instruction is the natural outflow of the "art" of teaching; to others, it is the disciplined labor of teaching as a "science." Designing learning experiences, as discussed in this chapter, really has much more to do with the art of relationships and community building than with the mere science of connecting pieces into a whole. The science is there, but often art is dominant.

Although not everyone will plan instruction in a sequential manner, it is useful to lay out a simple sequence of activities that flows logically from start to finish. In Figure 5:2, the main steps are connected with heavy arrows, indicating sequence; the light arrows indicate the interaction between the different steps while the creative process is under way.

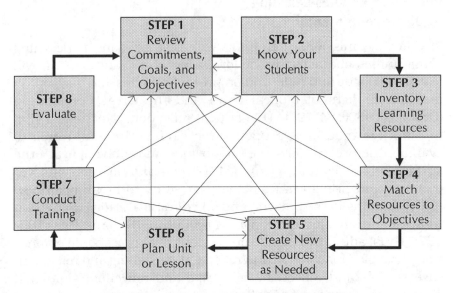

Figure 5:2. The Instructional Planning Sequence

1. The planning sequence which follows focuses on planning individual lessons or training sessions. Planning a training curriculum or a unit must precede planning learning experiences. Curriculum planning should be guided by principles of continuity, sequence, and integration. For an explanation of these principles, see Appendix F.

Step 1 – Review Commitments, Goals, and Objectives

It is wise to begin by reviewing your commitments and goals and by placing them foremost in your planning efforts. A review of the missionary or ministry profile is equally important to maintain a "big picture" perspective. In instructional design, it is too easy to "lose track of the forest for the trees."

While the big picture is important, we will not make significant headway toward designing learning experiences unless we also have our lesson objectives clearly in view. Reviewing these objectives is the last step in preparing ourselves to engage in lesson planning. Consider the following practical ways to review your objectives:

- *Review and focus.* Read over your commitments and training goals before spending time in prayer, alone and as a training team. Ask questions like these:
  - How do our training commitments inform our understanding of this objective?
  - How do our training goals inform our understanding of this objective?
  - What learning environment is most conducive to achieving this objective?
  - What specific learning activities will enable us to achieve this objective, understood in terms of our broader commitments and training goals?
- *Review and discuss.* Conducting this review with colleagues in a small group setting will allow members of the group to question and sharpen each other's thinking. In such a friendly setting, we can ask questions like these:
  - Are we clear and in agreement on what the *focus* of this unit or lesson should be?
  - Do we agree that the activities planned are appropriate to our objectives, goals, and commitments?
  - Are there other, more appropriate ways to accomplish our objectives than those we have planned?

Step 2 – Know Your Trainees

Transformational training focuses on the needs of trainees entering our programmes and attempts to customise the training to their level of education, skills, and maturity. This assessment can be done at application and entrance to our programmes through review of their experience, transcripts, and testimony. Assessment by trainers also continues throughout the training in order to see how the trainees are progressing. It is easy and natural to know one another when trainers and trainees are a part of "communities of learning."

There are two closely related reasons that knowing our trainees is essential. First, every learner is unique. Second, learning—especially formation—is relationally grounded. My wife, who teaches thirty fifth graders in our local public school, is constantly telling me stories of how important she finds it to draw on the divergent backgrounds, interests, and expertise of her elementary children. They represent eight ethnic groups, their parents range from poor to wealthy, some have travelled the world, and all bring a range of life experience that is fascinating. How much more important it is for missionary trainers to perceive their trainees as resources, as well as recipients.

Step 3 – Inventory Your Resources

Both scientists and artists are limited in their activities by the media available. Trainers can "broaden their vision" of what is available by recognising the resources that are readily available in their community—individuals, events, and places (historic, cultural, and religious). Be sure to include the resources of local congregations and affiliated mission agencies.

Jesus' model is instructive at this point. Review how his encounters with people—women, children, scribes, Pharisees, prophets, beggars, and lepers—were incorporated into his teaching. List the natural events of life—weddings, funerals, dinner parties, farming, eating, shopping, Sabbath observance, praying, tithing, and marketplace meetings—which he turned into training environments. Count the different places in which he taught—temple courtyards, private homes, markets, open fields, fishing boats, shaded hillsides, synagogues, and mountaintops. In the same way, trainers who know what is locally available can provide a richer mix of training experiences.

Step 4 – Match Resources to Objectives

You are now ready to determine what training activities best fit your learning objectives. You might adopt an existing activity, adapt a published learning experience, or combine several different activities into an integrated lesson. The key is to relate or link learning experiences and methods to the learning objectives you want to accomplish.

Each training activity should be designed to accomplish a specific training and development objective. The objectives you have written provide clues to appropriate methods and activities. To save time by focusing on the most powerful method to reach your objective is a matter of both stewardship *and* teaching effectiveness. What activities will achieve your objectives?

- *Start general; move to specifics.* Think in general terms initially to identify several alternative ways to achieve your objectives. Consider activities already going on in your area as identified in your inventory of local learning resources (see Step 3, above). Look at each activity to determine how well it will fit into your situation.

  - For example, if an objective says trainees will *analyse* the host culture, appropriate methods might include observation reports, field trips to ethnic neighbourhoods, case studies of people groups or cultures, and research and reports describing the designated culture.

- *Divide and match.* After looking over your broad goals and objectives for the entire unit, divide the learning into smaller, bite-sized parts for daily or hourly instruction.

- *Chart your objectives and experiences.* A chart is a useful display of objectives and possible learning experiences that can help you visually link or match different learning experiences to particular objectives. To use the worksheet in Figure 5:3, list your unit or lesson objectives in the left column. In column two, jot down any specific needs or characteristics of your trainees which may influence what you teach or how you teach it. In column three, list as

Learning Objectives	Trainees' Needs	Possible Learning Resources	Learning Experiences Selected
1.			
2.			
3.			

**Figure 5:3. Worksheet for Matching Resources
and Strategies to Objectives and Trainees**

many different and creative ways (i.e., methods and strategies) to accomplish each objective as you can, including what is available and what may need to be designed. In the fourth column, write only the learning experiences you will use to achieve each objective.

Once you have charted the information in this way, draw lines from the learning resources and activities on the right to the particular objective on the left that you think is the best "fit." This visual exercise will help you see which learning experiences you are using most often and which activities are not used at all.

In matching learning activities to training objectives, there are four tests which can be applied to guide the planning process. A simple checklist, like the one illustrated in Figure 5:4, can help you in applying these tests.

Checklist for Selecting Learning Activities

1. Is it appropriate:
   - to the training objective?
   - to the trainees' stage of development?
   - to the trainer's skills?
   - to the group size?
   - to the setting?
2. Is it learning focused?
3. Is it fresh?
4. Does it support all training commitments and goals?

Figure 5:4

1. Is it appropriate?

The nature of the training objectives, the knowledge, skill, character, and language level of the trainees, the abilities of the trainer, the size of the group, the size of the room or location of the setting, and the arrangement of the learning environment all influence the choice of methods and activities.

- Jesus led the twelve disciples on frequent field trips, interspersed with mini-lectures, demonstrations, and debriefing discussions. At other times, he lectured to thousands in the natural amphitheatres provided by hillsides. He waited until meal times for more intimate dialogues behind closed doors. His teaching method always matched his learning objective, taking into creative account the natural setting and the group size and composition.

Learning experiences must be appropriate to the trainees—neither too difficult nor too easy. The trainer should begin where the trainees are, not where he or she thinks they should be. Trainees cannot be stretched beyond their capabilities nor forced to go beyond their present abilities. The trainer must judge trainee readiness for the tasks to be performed.

- In the LAMP approach to language acquisition, students are urged to "Learn a little; use it a lot." This moves beginning language trainees into a variety of cross-cultural learning experiences appropriate to their present stage of development.

2. Is it learning focused?

In designing learning experiences which aid learning, *focus on the learner learning rather than on the teacher teaching.* A simple method to ensure focus on the trainees is to use a present participle (i.e., an "-ing" word) when specifying a method. Your description of the learning experience might read:

- In this unit, trainees are *analysing* case studies, *observing* village life, *interviewing* community members, *journalling*, *facilitating* discussions, *preaching* sermons, *teaching* lessons, *writing* reports, and *designing* community development projects.

Focusing on the trainee also means he or she must gain satisfaction from completing the behaviour implied by the objective. If the experiences selected are not enjoyable or if they are distasteful and unsatisfying, learning is less likely to occur.

- New missionary candidates can see the relevance of learning a new language, for example, when it helps them make new friends and do evangelism among their friends.

It usually is best to begin missionary training from the experiences of life. This is how Jesus most often began his teaching. When he didn't know people, he started right where they were. He began with people's questions and used those questions to stimulate growth. Jesus didn't immediately tell Nicodemus how to enter God's kingdom, but he aroused Nicodemus' curiosity and stimulated him to ask leading questions. Neither did Jesus tell the woman at the well that he was the Messiah until he actively involved her in thinking about physical water, living water, and true worship (Plueddemann 1990:56-57).

> Tell me and I'll forget;
> Show me and I may remember;
> Involve me and I'll understand.
> — Chinese proverb

3. Is it fresh?

In missionary training for cross-cultural ministry, trainers often use certain methods in frequent combination—observation and discussion, case study analysis and discussion, discovery and discussion, mini-lecture and application discussion, etc. Discussion may be the most common learning activity, but it should be used in different ways and in combination with various other "input" or discovery activities.

Traditionally, lecturing has been the most common method of presenting new information in a short amount of time. Lectured material is not always the most memorable, however, and lecturing can easily be supplemented by activities such as films, videos, role plays, and case studies which present new information in more "user friendly" ways.

4. Does it support all training commitments and goals?

Whenever we design learning experiences, we must be concerned about balancing all three dimensions at once—knowledge, skills, and character development. Although certain activities and experiences may focus on only one or two dimensions at a time, don't forget to include activities which integrate all of these dimensions.

Trainers facilitate true attitudinal and character change when they sensitively blend learning *about* God with genuine first-hand learning *from* God. This is done when trainers recognise the way in which truth must be felt and obeyed, as well as understood.

- Bob Pierce, the compassionate evangelist and founder of World Vision, moved by the needs of children orphaned by the Korean War, once prayed, "Let my heart be broken with the things that break the heart of God."

Every learning activity also must be consistent with the commitments which guide the training programme and with the programme's goals. A strategy which violates principles taught elsewhere in the training programme is always the wrong choice, irrespective of its efficiency in achieving a specific training objective.

Step 5 – Create New Resources as Needed

A range of training strategies exists. Ferris has pointed out, "The poverty of our individual repertoires is testimony to the effectiveness with which we allow our own experiences to limit our imagination and practice" (Ferris 1992:6). For missionary training to become more effective, the emerging generation of trainers and facilitators must develop more creative and diverse teaching methods than their predecessors.

It would be nice to be able to outline an easy-to-follow, step-by-step process for creating learning experiences that achieve our training objectives. Unfortunately, creativity cannot be reduced to a formula. Perhaps the most helpful stimulus to creativity is an appreciation of the range of training options available to the trainer and programme developer.

Missionary training strategies may be classed in two categories (Ferris 1992:6):

Classroom-Based Strategies	Field-Based Strategies
Lecture	Field observation and reflection
Dialogue	Trainer modelling and reflection
Case studies	Directed field assignments and reflection
Role play	Field ministry and reflection
Structured simulations	
Research and reflection	

Figure 5:5. Categories of Missionary Training Strategies

Traditionally, *classroom-based training* has relied on lecturing, answering questions, writing on the chalkboard, demonstrating, and showing audio-visual materials. Trainees worked individually by reading the text, solving problems, writing reports, using the library and other print resources, and sometimes by viewing films or videos or listening to tape recordings. Interaction between trainers and students and among students often took place by means of discussions and small group activities, student projects, and reports (Galvin and Veerman 1993:184).

Classroom-based learning experiences for adults also can include role plays, case studies, dramas, worksheets, games, simulations, projects, quizzes, presentations, small group work, stories, interviews, and skits. The list is almost endless. This process of creating and selecting learning experiences requires both artistry and careful evaluation. The critical concern for trainers is to select experiences which "fit" the learning objective.

For candidate and in-service training in spiritual maturity, classroom-based strategies could help in knowing *about* holiness without experiencing it. A *discipling* method and a *modelling-with-reflection* strategy that is situated in life and ministry, in the field or around the training centre, would be preferred.

In a *discipling strategy*, each candidate is mentored by a mature believer. Discipling will include Bible study, prayerful reflection, and discussion of character development goals as each quality is modelled by the discipler. This strategy necessitates life exposure between discipler and candidate. Two programmes which incorporate such discipling for developing spiritual maturity are the JIFU programme at China Graduate School of Theology (Hong Kong) and All Nations Christian College (Ware, Hertfordshire, UK). Without doubt, many other examples exist on each continent (cf. Ferris 1990).

Classroom-based instruction is a beneficial supplement to discipling, however. Classes on Missionary Life and Work, Missionary Biography, The Life of Christ, and Missionary Ministry in Acts are among many which afford opportunities to reflect on principles for Christian living and on historical models of holiness and spiritual power. To achieve character development goals, however, learning activities and reflection must focus on the character qualities to be developed.

For developing cross-cultural communication skills, *both* classroom-based *and* field-based strategies could be employed effectively. Classroom strategies may include case studies, role plays, and cultural simulations in addition to mini-lectures and discussions about the skills to be developed. Trainers must have extensive cross-cultural experience for effective personal illustration of the principles and skillful demonstration of the skills taught. Field-based strategies might include language learning forays into the surrounding community, venturing into the neighbourhood as "cultural detectives" to observe and reflect on what was seen, observing effective national communicators, and practicing non-verbal skills such as bowing, gesturing, and listening.

Field observation and field ministry opportunities might be jointly debriefed with reference to principles discussed in classroom studies. Frequent field trips to village and urban communities, as well as one or more extended immersions in field environments, will be beneficial to several areas of the curriculum, provided they are effectively debriefed.

Step 6 – Plan the Unit or Lesson

You are now ready to lay out your training plans. Planning learning activities for each session can be aided by using a "Lesson Planning Sheet" (see Appendix G). If you are just beginning to teach, this may seem like an unnecessary discipline. Over time, however, you will see yourself developing greater skill in shaping lessons which meet the needs of the trainees and which fulfill your training objectives.

A simple three-phase model is helpful for sequencing activities in a way which leads naturally from one phase to the next (Ward 1975).

Reflect

Start any learning experience (i.e., class, trip, or discussion) with a short time for reflection. Use simple exercises and activities which help trainees think about the topic, recall what they already know, and review their past experience related to the topic or issue. You can do these things by using one of the following activities:

- *Questions* – Have trainees write their response to a provocative opening question.
- *Quotes* – Have trainees think about the meaning of a striking quote.
- *Statistics* – Ask trainees to write for two minutes on their response to statistics.
- *One-page reflection sheets* – Use one-page handouts with questions, cases, or Bible passages for discussion.
- *Values clarifying exercises* – Have trainees rank the top ten values of their culture in contrast to the top values of the kingdom of God.
- *3" x 5" card reflection questions* – Have trainees write out on a 3" x 5" card their thoughts on an issue, topic, or dilemma.
- *Journal exercises* – Give trainees five minutes to record a recent lesson from God.

These and other activities can serve as "warm up" exercises for the mind, make trainees aware of how much they already know, and focus the trainees' concentration on the subject to be addressed.

Detect

During the second phase of the learning experience, trainers help the trainees discover new information, theories, and meanings for themselves, in addition to developing new skills and character traits. This phase focuses on helping the trainees learn new information or put information together in new and more meaningful ways.

A variety of different types of activities can be used to stimulate individual and group learning. "Input" methods range from the traditional lecture to discussions, games, simulations, forums, panels, question and answer periods, media starters, field trips, interviews, observation exercises, self-study modules, etc.

Project

In the third phase, trainees are helped to make *specific* application to their lives from the *general* kinds of learning gained. Trainees may be asked to think ahead, i.e., to *project* how the learning will apply, what changes they will need to make, what activity they will need to adjust or adapt, and to write guidelines or personal applications of theoretical principles.

"Project" activities include those which encourage and facilitate trainees' sharing with each other, such as buzz groups, brainstorming, question and answer, open-ended discussion, writing action plans, etc.

The goal of effective curriculum design encompasses much more than achieving individual training objectives. The greater goal is to equip whole people from the whole church to take the whole gospel to the whole world. In order for this goal to be accomplished effectively, missionary candidates need help integrating their learning into a cohesive fabric of biblical thinking and living. Trainers need to help trainees "re-connect" the pieces of their training experiences, synthesising the parts into a whole.

Step 7 – Conduct the Training

You will be eager to lead your training after having invested so much energy in planning your instruction. You soon will recognise how critical is the linkage between planning and instruction. Step-by-step planning can make the teaching-learning process seem simple and straight-forward. In reality, good teaching and effective learning can be extremely complex and messy. The complexity of learning (due to its relational nature) and our frailty in anticipating future interactions inevitably cause even the best instructional designs to fail if they are implemented woodenly.

Teaching is an active vocation, and professional teacher-trainers approach it interactively and reflectively. When we teach, we constantly "read" the class. We look for those who may not understand our instruction, who may be emotionally absent, who need to say something we didn't anticipate. We have learned to expect surprises. We must be willing to modify or abandon planned activities and objectives to pursue unanticipated learning opportunities. We often stop lecturing to follow up on a trainee's question. We allow a trainee's sharing of a recent experience to introduce a more immediate or relevant path toward our training goals. We talk, we listen, we weep, we laugh, we pray, we worship, and often none of these things were in our lesson plans. This approach is what Plueddemann (1991:3) calls "purposeful stumbling around."

The plan is a helpful starting place, nonetheless. Gifted trainers, after years of experience, may walk into a class with only a Bible and their life as the textbook. For most of us, however, lesson plans help us focus on what is important, on the principles to be learned in that session, and on how we will approach the topic at hand. Lesson planning is a tremendously helpful discipline for trainers to focus on instruction and to ensure that trainees' learning experiences match our training objectives.

Step 8 – Evaluate the Training

How will you assess the effectiveness of each learning experience and assure that learning is successful? On-going evaluation and adaptation can improve the effectiveness of any training plan and its component training experiences. Consider in advance how you will evaluate the effectiveness of each learning experience:

- What specific outcomes will you look for to determine success?
- Who will be responsible for assessment?
- When (by what date) will assessment be done?
- To whom does the observer or evaluator report?

View this final step of evaluation as a means of discovering how to improve. Don't get caught in the trap of thinking of evaluation as *assessing trainees*, as on a report card or as a pass/fail grade. You want to find out *how to be effective* in achieving *your training objectives*. Through trial and error experience, you will be able to determine which learning experiences are best suited to achieving your learning objectives and which experiences do not bring your trainees to your desired learning outcomes. Chapter 6 will provide more specific guidance for evaluating your lessons and your training programme.

Conclusion: Expanding the Range of Trainers' Roles and Abilities

Professional competence in teaching is an increased ability to fulfill a variety of roles effectively—including counsellor, facilitator, instructional manager, curriculum designer, academic instructor, evaluator, and mentor. A large part of teaching effectiveness consists in mastering the repertoire of approaches to teaching that are appropriate to those roles (LeFever 1990; Dettoni 1993:113-119). Joyce suggests that one's training "competence is expanded in two ways: first, by increasing the range of teaching strategies that we are able to employ; second, by becoming increasingly skillful in the use of these strategies" (Joyce 1978:3).

Unfortunately, there is no formula for matching learning activities to objectives. What may work for one trainer in one class or with one group of students can be unsatisfactory in another situation. You need to know the strengths and weaknesses of alternative methods and of various materials and curriculum. You will develop this familiarity through experimentation and practice. Then you can make your selection in terms of the student characteristics and needs that will *best* serve the objectives you have established.

Practise what you have learned by doing Exercise 5:1 on the next page, "Identifying and Designing Learning Experiences."

Exercise 5:1
Identifying and Designing Learning Experiences

1. Inventory: List the types of learning experiences that are currently used in your training centre or programme.

2. Select *four* learning experiences that are used most often and evaluate the effectiveness of each in terms of your programme's purpose, goals, and/or objectives.

Learning Experience	Effectiveness
a.	
b.	
c.	
d.	

3. Identify at least three *additional* learning experiences which might teach the competencies for which you wrote learning objectives in Exercise 4:1 (pages 82-83).

a.

b.

c.

4. From the learning experiences listed in #2 and #3 above, identify *five* experiences which promise to have the fewest negative consequences and the most positive outcomes in your cultural setting. Be prepared to explain your list to a colleague.

a.

b.

c.

d.

e.

Chapter 6

Evaluating Training Outcomes

Robert Ferris

It is common for non-educators to view programme development as a start-up activity, something which must be tackled once, at the outset of a new training programme. Anyone involved in training, on the other hand, understands that programme development is an on-going process. To remain vital, relevant, and effective, training programmes must continue to develop.

Evaluation is the step which closes the loop on programme development. As set forth in this manual, programme development begins with clarifying training commitments, then employs a two-step process (including developing a ministry profile) to identify training goals. The programme of training becomes real when goals are distilled into specific objectives and are implemented through planned and structured experiences. We can't stop there, though. We need to observe the effect of our training and ask how the training can be improved. This is the task of evaluation. By assessing training outcomes and identifying implications for future instruction, evaluation closes the programme development loop. A disciplined review of training experiences and outcomes can assist in the reconsideration of commitments, training goals, training objectives, and training strategies.

Three Aspects of Evaluation

Any evaluation should attend to three distinct aspects of the training programme: training processes, training outcomes, and stewardship of resources.

Training processes include all the intentional activities and relationships by which the training programme seeks to shape the understanding, skills, and character of the trainee. This may include trainee selection, in-class instruction, on-campus training (e.g., survival, sanitation, health, gardening, construction, homemaking, mechanical skills), in-field training (e.g., community orientation, evangelism, church planting), trainer demonstration or modelling, discipling or mentoring, cultural immersion, internships, group worship and prayer, recreation, community life, personal counselling, and ministry or career guidance. Please note that this list is intended to be suggestive, rather than exhaustive; the training processes evaluated for any programme should be those employed by the programme.

When training processes have been identified, each should be examined for consistency with the programme's training commitments and goals and for stewardship of the programme's resources. A simple table (see Figure 6:1) which provides ample space for recording observations and findings can simplify this task.

To use this table, list training processes in the first column, comment on the appropriateness of each process factor in the second column, and record conclusions and recommendations in the third column.

Training Process	Commentary on Consistency with Commitments, Goals, and Stewardship	Satisfaction Level and Recommended Steps to Improvement
Trainee selection		
In-class instruction		
[Etc.]		

Figure 6:1. Sample Table for Recording
Process Evaluation Findings

There are two kinds of *training outcomes*, each of which requires a different method of evaluation. *Intended outcomes* should be assessed in terms of training goals and objectives. If training goals have been specified (as described in Chapter 3) and if lesson objectives have been defined (as described in Chapter 4), this is a straight-forward exercise. As in the case of programme processes, however, a table can simplify the task (see Figure 6:2).

Standard (Commitment, Goal, or Objective)	Evidence of Attainment (Pro and Con)	Satisfaction Level and Recommended Steps to Improvement
Objectives determined by standards of performance		
Training is church-related and community-based		
[Etc.]		

Figure 6:2. Sample Table for Recording Intended Outcome Evaluation Findings

Use this table like the previous one. List training goals (or lesson objectives) in column one, then enter evidence of goal or objective attainment in column two. Since it is rare for all goals to be attained with equal effectiveness, the third column should record observations and recommendations to improve the training programme.

Unintended outcomes are quite different from intended outcomes. Although any individual or group activity—especially an activity as complex as teaching and learning—has unanticipated effects, these often are overlooked by inexperienced evaluators. In fact, however, unintended outcomes can delightfully enhance or tragically mitigate the effects of a programme which, in systems terms, attains all (or most) of its stated objectives.

- A "slum living" experience was designed to teach mission-ary trainees skills needed for survival in urban ministry situations. Annually, however, the training staff observed that the weeks spent in the slums produced strong friendship bonding among trainees which persisted throughout the balance of the training programme and into their missionary careers.

One danger of identifying specific objectives for training is a tendency to produce a kind of "tunnel vision." Like individuals without peripheral vision, we see only what we are looking at. Like them, also, our greatest jeopardy or blessing may lie just outside this narrow field of vision. To resolve that problem, we need deliberately to broaden our area of focus. Instead of looking only at goal attainment, we need to ask, "What *other* positive or negative effects is our training producing?"

Just asking that question is the first step in the evaluation of unintended outcomes. The question itself is also crucial. Only as we recognise the unintended outcomes of our training can we adjust our training plans to capitalise on and enhance positive outcomes or to diminish or eliminate negative outcomes.

The procedure for evaluating unintended outcomes is like that for evaluating programme processes. First a list of unintended outcomes, both positive and negative, must be developed. This may involve brainstorming by the training staff, polling current trainees and alumni, and interviewing constituent church and mission leaders. When a responsible list has been assembled, the outcomes identified should be examined against the programme's commitments and training goals. (A table similar to Figure 6:1 is very useful, but instead of listing training processes in column one, list the unintended outcomes that have been identified.) Often the evaluation of unanticipated outcomes leads to the most significant insights toward immediate programme improvement.

Finally, evaluators must consider the programme's **stewardship of resources**. As Christians, we own nothing; everything we have is held in trust for God. We are stewards; we are held accountable for the way we use the resources entrusted to us. Again, we need to think broadly. Resources include financial resources and physical resources (land, buildings, and equipment), but also personnel resources and environmental resources. A few minutes' reflection usually will yield a respectable list of individuals, organisations, and points of cultural or religious interest existing in the environs of the training centre which can be used to strengthen missionary training.

Evaluation Procedures

Any procedure which enables us to reflect knowledgeably on training in terms of our commitments, training goals, and stewardship of resources qualifies as "programme evaluation." Although the time and energy invested in evaluation will vary, it is useful to consider the variety of strategies available to programme evaluators, whether the evaluators are programme staff or an external individual or team.

Tests of trainees' knowledge or skills are the most commonly employed means of evaluating effectiveness and the attainment of training goals and objectives. Whenever tests are employed, evaluators should assure that the information or skills tested are consistent with stated learning objectives. It also is important for trainers and evaluators to recognise, however, that tests administered at the training centre afford only an indirect and intermediate measure of trainees' readiness for ministry. The ultimate goal of information and skill training is the formation of Christian character and life-long, growing effectiveness in ministry.

Exhibits, such as trainer or trainee portfolios or products demonstrating trainee skills, afford a second evidence of training programme effectiveness. A garden can provide convincing evidence of trainees' mastery of cultivation principles. A garment sewn by a trainee can demonstrate the effectiveness of preparation for "self-supporting" ministries. A tape recording of a sermon preached by a trainee, or a Bible study taught, can effectively document mastery of preaching and teaching skills. Likewise, a doctrinal statement developed by a trainee can evidence his or her grasp of basic Christian truths. When several similar exhibits, produced by different trainees, are examined, evaluators can observe the effectiveness of the training programme.

Direct inquiry methods include interviews and questionnaires. Generally interviews are preferred, except when the persons to be questioned are widely distributed geographically or when the number of individuals is relatively large. Often direct inquiry methods are the most useful way to obtain information about persons and their opinions. Direct inquiry may be used to collect self-reports, peer reports (i.e., reports by one or more friends), trainer or supervisor reports, and congregational or ministry team reports (i.e., collective judgments in ministry contexts). Since character qualities are not accessible to testing or exhibition, direct inquiry is almost the only means for assessing attainment of character development goals. Congregational or ministry team reports, along with trainer or supervisor reports, also provide a useful index of ministry skill development. We sometimes have felt that we could learn more about a training programme by interviewing four alumni in their ministry setting than by spending four days at the training centre!

Finally, some aspects of a training programme can be assessed only by *direct observation*. Especially when evaluating programme processes and stewardship of resources, evaluators may need to observe training procedures, interpersonal relations, institutional records,[1] physical facilities (i.e., buildings and equipment), and environmental resources.

Two Types of Evaluation

There are two ways we can evaluate training: through on-going evaluation and periodic evaluation. On-going evaluation provides a stream of information, sometimes imprecise and often informal, on training effectiveness. Periodic evaluation, on the other hand, affords a larger and more systematic assessment of training programme effectiveness. For most training programmes, it probably is not useful to schedule periodic evaluation more often than once in five to seven years. If your programme is seven years old and you have not conducted a periodic evaluation, however, we believe you would find this a valuable discipline. This chapter will provide guidance for conducting on-going and periodic evaluations of missionary training.

On-going Evaluations

Evaluation may occur at any point in a training programme, and it probably should. Most commonly, however, we evaluate our training daily, at the end of each training unit, and at the conclu-

---

1. Institutional records examined may include any or all of the following: official documents and minutes, policy statements, staff personnel records, trainee admission records, trainee assessment reports, alumni records, financial records and statements, income and development plans, and property development and maintenance plans.

sion of each programme cycle. To be sure, the formality of these evaluations may differ, but the means employed are similar and the criteria applied are the same.

Daily, following each training session, a wise trainer will ask himself or herself, "How did it go today?" This is the time to make notes on parts of the lesson which were particularly effective or ineffective, including especially positive experiences or insightful discussions, problems encountered by trainees, illustrations which did not illustrate, demonstrations or explanations which require more clarity, etc. Daily evaluation typically depends on the trainer's subjective assessment of the training experience in light of the commitments which guide training and the objectives set for the day. Trainers who take time to make such notes, however, will find them invaluable aids to future preparation.

Assessment *at the end of each training unit* (lectureship, internship, course, or term) often is more formal. Usually some measure of trainee achievement (e.g., a grade, fluency level, etc.) is part of unit completion. While we typically view these measures as assessments of the trainees, it is helpful to view them as assessments of training effectiveness as well. Assuming that admission standards are appropriate, effective training should result in high levels of trainee achievement. When trainees fail to learn, it is safe to conclude the trainer has failed also. It is useful, furthermore, to supplement records of trainee achievement with the trainer's assessment of the unit's success vis-à-vis training commitments and unit objectives.

It is also helpful to request trainees to evaluate each unit of the training programme as the unit is completed. We recommend an evaluation form that lists training commitments and asks trainees to rate (from high to low on a 5-point scale) how effectively each commitment was demonstrated in this unit. A second section of the evaluation form lists unit objectives and asks trainees to rate the extent to which the training achieved each objective. A third section may list specific topics or activities included in the unit, requesting assessment of their effectiveness in promoting unit objectives. We also have found it useful to include a fourth section, in which trainees are invited to provide any additional comments or suggestions. Often trainees have nothing to add, but at other times this fourth section will yield the most encouraging or most insightful feedback.[2]

Usually student evaluations confirm the trainer's subjective assessment, but occasionally students will identify weak areas of which the trainer is unaware. Trainers who are unaccustomed to trainee evaluations may find this practice unsettling. Nevertheless, by submitting ourselves to trainee evaluation, we demonstrate a willingness to humble ourselves to learn from our trainees. Besides the insights gained for strengthening our training programmes, trainee evaluations provide a strong positive example for our trainees.

At the conclusion of each programme cycle, usually annually, it is worthwhile for the training staff to review the cycle as a whole, assessing the staff's faithfulness to training commitments and their achievement of programme goals. The conclusion of a programme cycle provides a particularly appropriate occasion for a global review of the training programme. Reflection on the ministry preparedness of the recent graduates affords the training staff an opportunity to assess the outcome of their training in very specific ways. By discussing the effectiveness of each unit of the programme and the interaction of those units, training staff can gain insight for improving the programme units or for refining the training programme as a whole.

Every healthy training programme has a systematic plan of on-going evaluation. This is the staff's only means of assuring that areas of weakness are identified and addressed and that programme improvement is continuous. Methods may vary, but on-going evaluation always is oriented to three considerations: (1) faithfulness to programme commitments, (2) achievement of programme objectives, and (3) stewardship of programme resources. On-going evaluation provides the shortest and surest route to programme improvement.

---

2. A sample evaluation form which illustrates this pattern is provided in Appendix H.

Periodic Evaluation

Occasionally it is useful to step back from our training programmes, to look at them holistically in a fresh light, to attempt to see them as others do. Formal programme evaluation is a science. Although various approaches exist, the one which best fits the commitments and values of ministry trainers has been termed "responsive evaluation."[3] This approach is responsive in that evaluation is concerned with the responses of various groups of people affected by the training programme.

Responsive evaluation proceeds from a set of assumptions which ministry trainers can endorse. Its view of reality is holistic, its stance is participative, its goal is programme improvement, its interest is to learn from human responses and assessments, and its assumptions are sensitive to moral and educational values (Guba and Lincoln 1983:313-323).

Definition of Terms

Before proceeding to a description of this approach to periodic evaluation, three terms must be defined and five groups distinguished. Although periodic evaluation need not be complex, it will be helpful to clarify our use of terms at the outset.[4]

"Merit" is the presence of values affirmed broadly among educators of a particular type—in our case, missionary trainers. Where shared values have been codified, as in lists of accreditation standards, assessment of "merit" is quite straight-forward. Missionary trainers rarely have reflected collectively on the values and commitments which direct their training programmes.[5] In the absence of a more broadly based statement of values, the training

---

3. This term was coined by Stake (1983). The same model is sometimes identified as "naturalistic evaluation" because of its attention to interactions in natural contexts (Guba and Lincoln 1983). See Appendix I for a broader view of educational programme evaluation.

4. The concepts and language described are drawn from the sources cited in the paragraph above, with one exception. "Integrity" is a factor recognised by a team of educators appointed to develop a scheme for accrediting TEE in Asia (Ferris and others 1986). Ferris (1989) has provided a full description of that project.

5. Such a project is under way in India (Swamidoss 1994).

programme's own commitments, clarified and owned through the process described in Chapter 1 of this manual, can be used.

"Worth" is the presence of values specific to one programme and its context. These values are the factors which make one missionary training programme distinct. "Worth" includes, but goes beyond, the stated goals of a training programme. "Worth" is a function of the needs and expectations of a training programme's constituency—the churches, mission agencies, and individuals it serves. The "worth" of a training programme also relates to the programme's appropriateness to the cultural contexts from which trainees come and into which they will be sent.

"Integrity" relates to the way the periodic evaluation is conducted. It is the appropriateness of the procedures employed and the seriousness with which the evaluation is pursued.

In addition to these terms, we also need to identify five groups who are significant to the periodic evaluation process.

The *training centre staff* is the community of trainers who staff the missionary training centre. In some cases the centre staff may be known as the centre's "faculty." Generally both full-time and part-time trainers are considered centre staff. It usually is not helpful to consider as staff non-residential trainers who participate only occasionally in the centre's training programmes.

The *centre administrator* bears responsibility for directing the daily operation of the training centre. Sometimes the centre administrator is known as the centre's "director," "principal," "dean," or "president." Although she or he may function as "first among equals," the centre staff are responsible to the centre administrator.

The *centre's board of directors or trustees* are a small group of mature Christian individuals, external to the training centre but committed to its mission, to whom the centre administrator is responsible. If the training centre is operated by a church, a denomination, or a mission agency, the centre's board may be a committee charged with oversight of the training centre. Even when the training centre is organised as an independent ministry, it is generally accepted that the centre administrator needs a clearly identified group to whom she or he can look for accountability and advice. If the training centre is an independent ministry, the centre's board may be a legally constituted body. When legally constituted, the board may hold title to any property belonging to the training centre and may be responsible for appointing the centre administrator and the staff. Usually it is not advisable for members of the administrator's extended family or for training centre staff to serve on the centre's board of directors or trustees.

The *evaluation team* consists of two or three persons, including one from the training centre staff, who are charged with conducting the periodic evaluation. At least one member of the evaluation team should be familiar with the procedures of social research. To avoid conflicts of interest, the centre administrator should not be appointed to the evaluation team.

The *evaluation guidance committee* is a group representative of the training centre's stakeholders.[6] It is convenient for the evaluation guidance committee to be no larger than necessary. Usually one carefully selected representative of each stakeholding group is satisfactory. The centre staff is a stakeholding group and should be represented on the evaluation guidance committee.

The Evaluation Procedure

A periodic evaluation of the training centre's programme can be pursued as a ten-step process.

1. The decision to conduct a periodic evaluation should be taken by the centre's board of directors or trustees. It may be necessary, however, for the centre administrator to recommend that a periodic evaluation is needed. When the board authorises evaluation of the training centre's programmes, it also should appoint the evaluation team.

2. The first task of the evaluation team is to identify the training programme's stakeholder groups. The centre's board, administrator, and staff should be consulted regarding the list of stakeholders, since the credibility of the evaluation will be diminished if any significant stakeholder group is overlooked. At the same time, it is advisable to identify an individual, as well as an alternate, who can represent the interests of each stakeholding group. (The alternate will be needed only in the event that the

---

6. The concept of "stakeholder" was introduced in Chapter 2. Readers who are not familiar with this term may find it useful to review that section before proceeding.

original individual is unable to serve.) These stakeholder representatives, when recruited, will constitute the evaluation guidance committee.

3. The evaluation team should call a meeting of the evaluation guidance committee. The agenda of this meeting is to identify factors relevant to the "worth" of the training programme. After the stated training goals of the centre are reviewed, each member of the committee should address (a) the perceived purpose of the training centre; (b) issues or concerns related to the design, operation, or impact of the training programmes; and (c) sources of evidence perceived to relate to the effectiveness of the training centre in meeting the needs and expectations of the representative's stakeholding group. With various perceptions on the table, it then is the task of the evaluation guidance committee to negotiate any differences in order to produce a coherent statement of factors relevant to the "worth" of the training programme. This is essential to the continuing work of the evaluation team.

4. The evaluation team next must develop a strategy for assessing the training programme's stated objectives, its "merit," and its "worth." The evaluation team should be assured full and uninhibited access to all records maintained by the training centre. Survey or interview data collected from the training administrator and staff, current trainees, alumni of the training centre, and selected stakeholder groups will be critical to the evaluation. Special attention also should be given to sources of evidence identified by members of the evaluation guidance committee in their first meeting.

5. A second meeting of the evaluation guidance committee should be called to review the evaluation strategy developed by the evaluation team. Following presentation of the proposed strategy, discussion should focus on the adequacy of the strategy and any adjustments which may be required. At the close of this meeting, the evaluation guidance committee should assure the evaluation team that the amended strategy is an acceptable approach to assessment of the training programme. If this is impossible, steps 4 and 5 must be repeated.

6. The evaluation team should proceed with the evaluation, according to the strategy approved by the evaluation guidance committee. Findings should be analysed, and a report should be

prepared addressing the training centre's achievement of its stated objectives, and the "worth" and "merit" of the training programme. The evaluation team also should identify any adjustments in personnel, facilities, or programme design which are indicated by their findings.

7. A third meeting of the evaluation guidance committee should be called to review the evaluation team's report. The evaluation team should present its report section by section, allowing opportunity for members of the evaluation guidance committee to question the team's findings, interpretations, or recommendations. Objections raised by any member of the evaluation guidance committee must be addressed by the evaluation team and by the committee as a whole. If added perspective permits reinterpretation of the evidence collected, and if this new interpretation is acceptable to all members of the evaluation guidance committee, the report may be amended in that meeting. If any member objects to the way evidence was collected or interpreted or to the sources from which evidence was drawn, the evaluation team either must defend its procedure to the satisfaction of the committee or must collect additional evidence which addresses the stated concerns. When the evaluation guidance committee is satisfied that the report of the evaluation team accurately reflects the "merit" and "worth" of the training programme, the committee's work is done.

8. The evaluation team should review its report, as approved by the evaluation guidance committee, with the training centre administrator and the training centre staff. Unlike the evaluation guidance committee, the training centre administrator and staff do not have the prerogative to require amendment of the evaluation report, although any overlooked information should be noted. This review is provided as a courtesy to the administrator and staff, inasmuch as they will be responsible for implementing any recommendations included in the report which are mandated by the training centre board.

9. The evaluation team should draft a statement on the "integrity" of the evaluation project, describing the procedures and strategies employed and specifically noting and justifying any deviations from the approach outlined here.

10. The evaluation team should present its full report, addressing the "merit" and "worth" of the training programme and the "integrity" of the evaluation project, to the training centre's board of directors or trustees.

When the evaluation team's report has been received by the training centre's board, the team's work is completed. The board, then, is responsible to determine which of the recommendations included in the report should be implemented and to provide for their implementation.

Although this process may appear complex, in practice it can function very smoothly. The most difficult problems are encountered when various stakeholding groups hold deeply divergent understandings of the centre's purpose. Despite the complexity of negotiating these differences, the training centre cannot be successful in the midst of such division. In such a case, *achieving a common understanding of the training centre's mission may be the most significant product of the evaluation.* When differences exist, it is critical to the work of the evaluation team that they avoid taking sides; they may facilitate the negotiation, but they must not "get caught in the middle." The stakeholders themselves must resolve any differences; then the evaluation team may proceed on the basis of the negotiated understandings.

Much will depend on appointing the right persons to the evaluation team and on providing them the time and resources needed to do their work. It is not realistic to expect members of the evaluation team to fulfill their responsibilities while maintaining a full workload. The budget required to underwrite the evaluation project will depend on the geographic distribution of the members of the evaluation guidance committee and on the evaluation strategies employed. If travel expenses of the evaluation guidance committee members can be minimised, and if the evaluation team can collect its data without extensive travel (e.g., by sampling alumni opinion via postal survey, rather than personal interviews), periodic evaluation need not be expensive. It is unrealistic, however, to assume that evaluation can be cost free.

The costs of periodic evaluation must be weighed against the benefits it affords. Periodic evaluation is the most effective way to assure that the training centre is fulfilling its mission and is serving well its various stakeholders. Periodic evaluation also is the most effective way to identify areas in which the training centre's programmes can and should be improved. Another way to say this is, the periodic evaluation provides information which is essential to the on-going development of the missionary training programme. We have never encountered a training programme board which regretted the time and resources invested in a periodic evaluation, but we know of several which have made significant adjustments in training programmes on the basis of information obtained through a periodic evaluation using the process described here.

Conclusion

When training is not evaluated, training centre administrators and staff have no informed basis on which to improve their programmes. Programme evaluation, however, "closes the loop" on programme development. In this chapter we have described procedures for both on-going and periodic evaluations. In both types of evaluation, training outcomes are compared with training goals, and training methods are compared with training commitments. Periodic evaluation broadens the scope of inquiry to assure that the training centre's stakeholders are well served. The findings of programme evaluation afford perspective for reassessing training commitments and programme goals. Thus, the programme development "loop" is closed, and the way is opened for continuing, significant improvement of missionary training.

CHAPTER 7

STARTING A MISSIONARY TRAINING PROGRAMME

Lois Fuller

As the church around the world awakens to its global responsibility to fulfill the Great Commission, missionaries are volunteering for service from countries that have not had missionary training programmes in the past. Often the first missionaries have struggled and even failed because of problems that good training might have enabled them to avoid or resolve. Now, missionary training programmes are being started in many countries around the world. This manual raises considerations and presents information needed by people leading missionary training programmes. The preceding chapters addressed issues related to curriculum planning, but this chapter will look at matters of planning and administration. We hope this manual will be useful both to those starting new missionary training programmes and to those evaluating and improving existing programmes.

Before You Start

Everyone on the training committee was sure that a missionary training school was a terrific idea. They asked around to find out how such schools were run in other places. Then they tried to do the same in their own area. Six months later, when their training programme closed in failure, no one could understand why. They were sure they had provided thorough publicity, a great curriculum, and wonderful resources, but they just could not seem to attract enough students. What could the training committee have

121

done differently to assure that their programme would meet the training needs of the greatest number of students?

Determining Who Is Responsible for Training

The Great Commission was given to the church. The task of world evangelisation belongs to the church. Training personnel for the task of world evangelisation—missionary training—therefore, also belongs to the church. While God may use an individual or a small group of individuals to excite others with a vision for missionary training, it is important to recognise that successful missionary training never can be a private project.

When God lays a burden for missionary training on the heart of one or more believers, it is important for them, first of all, to seek to win others to that vision. Those in leadership roles within the church and leaders of missionary sending agencies should be among the first to be challenged with the need for effective missionary training.

Two things are needed in order to implement a successful missionary training programme. First, the project must be the fruit of incessant prayer. "The prayer of a righteous man is powerful and effective" (Jas 5:16)! Second, those who challenge others to share their vision for missionary training must be well informed about the task they expect to undertake. Some initial research may be needed in order to identify clearly the need which exists. Great care should be taken, however, since research always begins with assumptions and leads to decisions. The earlier that leaders from the church and missionary sending agencies join in this process, the greater their sense of *participation* and *ownership* will be. As the missionary training programme is shaped by the collective wisdom of many godly men and women, the viability and effectiveness of the programme will be enhanced.

How large a group should share the vision for a missionary training programme before specific planning is begun? The answer must vary with the goals of the envisioned programme, the trainees it will prepare, and its formal relationship to missionary sending organisations—the local congregations, church denominations, and independent mission agencies which send and support cross-cultural missionaries. It is essential, however, that the resulting missionary training programme is viewed by ourselves and others as a cooperative ministry of the church and not as a project of one or a few individuals. We will have more to say about this point later in this chapter.

Establishing the Need
for a Missionary Training Programme

In the commercial world, when a company wants to launch a new product, they do market research to predict whether people will buy the product. A commercial company exists to make money, so research is designed to find out if a new product will bring a profit. The aim of missionary training, in contrast, is to see many unreached individuals and people groups evangelised and discipled as followers of Jesus Christ. Training will not be successful if trainees are not gifted and called to missionary service, if too few missionaries are trained, or if training does not equip people to be effective missionaries.

If there are other missionary training programmes available in your area, find out more about them. What are their training goals? For what level of involvement in missions are they preparing people? Where do they get students? How are they run? Are they serving well the church of Jesus Christ and its missionaries? Can you combine efforts, in order to avoid expensive duplication of resources and to strengthen the ministry of other programmes?

Are there groups of people who would be interested in missions but who, for some reason, cannot take advantage of existing missionary training? Perhaps a certain kind of training is not available. If a new programme is needed, it should aim at meeting the training needs of a neglected group.

The missionary training of Youth With a Mission (YWAM) is an example of this philosophy. YWAM targets people without formal theological training, perhaps without the means or time to go through the long preparation required by most Western missions, people who are nonetheless interested in missionary service. By providing short, segmented training without heavy academic prerequisites, YWAM has recruited and trained a vast army for the evangelisation of the world. They could never have done this if they had just started another Bible college.

People come to a missionary training programme because they or their sponsoring agencies recognise a need for training. They will come, however, only if the costs in time, opportunity, and money are affordable. They might not finish the training if it does not hold their interest or meet their needs. Research should be designed to answer two questions:

- Who are the people who recognise a need (or should and could be taught to recognise a need) for missionary training?
- How can training be offered so that potential trainees are able and willing to take advantage of it?

If your research reveals that missionary training programmes that are currently available are serving the church well and are meeting the training needs which exist, perhaps your training committee should concentrate its efforts on strengthening one of the existing programmes, rather than trying to amass the resources to start something new.

Determining the Type of Training Needed

There are various aspects to missions education. Pre-candidate programmes cater especially to people who are not missionaries but who want to know more about missions. These programmes enable people to pray and give to missions, and some trainees will be encouraged to go further and to prepare for missionary service. Other missionary training programmes train recognised missionary candidates, and some programmes are designed to provide in-service training for missionaries who already have been on the field.

Prospective trainees for pre-candidate training include all Christians, since all should be interested in the Great Commission. Often, however, pre-candidate training is designed for prospective missionaries. These may include Christian students (in both secular and theological institutions), Christian young people who have left (or never attended) school, and older Christians who are challenged to change or modify their careers in order to become missionaries. Such people are found in church or ministry groups, theological schools, and campus fellowships. These groups may be surveyed to find out how many individuals are interested in learning about missions or about how to be missionaries. How many of them sense some kind of missionary call? Researchers should ask about topics of interest and times available for missions training. Perhaps these Christians are not ready to devote their full time to missions study, even for a short term. Maybe one-day seminars or correspondence courses would draw the most response from them.

In Western countries, people who want to become missionaries usually look for training on their own. They attend a Bible college or seminary and take a missions programme. Later they apply to a mission agency to be sent out. Many agencies do not accept candidates unless they already have most of their training. The agencies expect the Bible colleges and seminaries to do the training.

In other parts of the world, however, candidates often join a missionary sending organisation before training. Many churches, denominations, and independent mission agencies will not recognise training done outside the advice and supervision of their organisation. They require the candidate to undergo training under their supervision, even if the candidate was trained elsewhere. When mission-directed training is expected, we may waste our time if we train people who are not under appointment by a sending organisation. Unappointed trainees may find no way to use their training unless they serve independently or start their own sending organisation. If we ignore the relationship of trainees to sending organisations, few of our trainees may go on to be successful missionaries.

If a candidate training programme is expected to serve prospective missionaries from several sending organisations, it is useful to make a list of local congregations, church denominations, and independent mission agencies which are or may be sending out missionaries. Find out whether these organisations would be interested in sending their candidates to a joint training programme. How long would they like such training to last? Would they prefer to send students only for short seminars or for training programmes lasting a few months, a year, or longer? How many candidates might they have available to send in the next year or the next few years? Would the sending organisations recognise the training of candidates who had gone through the joint programme before applying for missionary appointment? If so, missionary trainers could recruit potential missionaries and train them, expecting the agencies to appoint them to service.

Many times local congregations, church denominations, and independent mission agencies want to bond candidates to their own organisation and immerse them in their own vision and ethos. They might not be willing to release candidates to a joint training programme for a long period of time. They are happy to send candidates for short seminars and courses of up to about three months but not for a year or more. Sometimes these sending organisations have not consciously formed their training policies and are not able to explain to us how they really feel. We may have to experiment with different lengths of training to see where the greatest response comes. Training that takes several years may have to be done mainly by sending organisations rather than by joint training programmes.

Sending organisations also should be surveyed about the missionaries they have on the field. Would these missionaries appreciate in-service or refresher courses? On what topics? For how long? At what time?

If a training programme is set up for a single sending organisation, the organisation will recruit candidates and will assign them to the training programme. It is quite likely that the organisation will send out the trainees when they finish training, so there is less danger that they will lack an opportunity to do missionary work. The sending organisation can keep the candidate in training as long as necessary, depending on the trainee's background, maturity, motivation, and clarity of vision. Training can be adapted more easily to tasks and opportunities in the mission. This is true especially in an organisation that has work within its own country. A single organisation training programme often will work harder at spiritual formation. Since the sending organisation expects to work permanently with the candidate, it has a greater stake in the individual's character.

The Need for Prayer

The ultimate reason for missionary training is to make disciples of all nations, filling heaven with worshippers, in obedience to our Lord's command. We must have no other agenda than this. It is his work, and it becomes ours only because we have joined ourselves to him. All our plans and research are auxiliaries to prayer. We ask the Lord for his direction about missionary training in our situation. He leads us to information sources and shows us the significance of our research findings. He gives us his vision for what should be done, and wisdom for all the decisions that must be made along the way. It must be supernatural work from first to last.

The Context

Before deciding on things like programme goals, facilities, and curriculum, it is important to look at the context in which missionary training will be conducted. Several groups of people (missionary sending organisations, teachers, students, missionary co-workers, funding organisations, and receiving churches) will be directly affected by decisions made regarding the missionary training programme. These people are sometimes called the "stakeholders" of the programme. They stand to gain or lose by how the programme is run, and they can affect its outcomes. It is not necessary for all stakeholders to be represented on the training committee. The training committee should consist of persons who share the vision for missionary training and who are committed to meeting the missionary training needs of the church. Those on the training committee must be sensitive to all stakeholders and must seek to win the allegiance of stakeholders to the tasks of world evangelism and missionary training.

There also are environments to be considered: the location of the training programme, the background of the mission trainees, and the mission fields in which the trainees are likely to work. All these context factors affect decisions about many aspects of the programme. They must be identified and analysed. The answers to the questions below will help your training committee determine how plans for the programme should be made.

Who are the people to be trained?

Do they already have some theological training? What is their theological orientation (pentecostal, fundamentalist)? What is their secular educational background? From what ethnic group or groups are they? What are their cultural values and economic levels? Will families be involved as well as individuals? Men as well as women? What will be their age range? What skills and occupations do they already have? What will the trainees expect to gain from the programme? Will they be satisfied with the outcomes?

Often, until trainees appear, we cannot be sure of the answers to all of these questions, but we can try to predict. The answers will affect some of the informal training that will take place outside class whether we like it or not (for example, trainees may try to influence each other theologically). Sometimes we will have to plan how to minimise any undesirable results. For example, if ethnic groups with traditional animosity are to be mixed, how can love be fostered? The characteristics of the trainees will also determine in part how effective certain teaching methods will be and how necessary it will be to include some things in the curriculum while other things can be assumed to be already understood.

What kind of co-workers will the trainees likely have?

In some parts of the world, most of the students will be working with international sending organisations, where their missionary co-workers may have a different culture and mother tongue. These students will need help in coping with the cross-cultural element inside the mission. Other programmes will train missionaries whose co-workers all share their own background. All trainees still need skills in getting along with their colleagues.

In what mission fields are the trainees likely to work?

Especially at the beginning, our programme will not likely be able to train students for every potential mission field. At first it may be that the missionaries we train will work mainly with unreached groups in our own part of the world. We might not need to teach Hinduism in a training programme in West Africa, for instance, if the students will be targeting unreached African tribes. Training for those who will work in remote rural areas should include practical things that may not be needed by urban missionaries and vice versa. The necessary survival and health skills for those reaching Eskimos in the cold north will be somewhat different from those needed by people working in the tropics. Language learning techniques needed for various fields may be different. Some countries are strict about letting in only missionaries who are perceived as (academically or professionally) "qualified." Should missionary training help them gain that status? If yes, how? Is there a receiving church whose voice should be heard about the kind of missionaries that would be of most help to them?

What sending organisations will be served by the training?

Sending groups must be taken into consideration. Do they include local congregations, church denominations, and independent mission agencies? How does their administrative structure affect their relationship to the programme? Do they agree with the philosophy and curriculum of the programme? If several sending organisations are to use the programme together, will some be afraid of trainees' switching over from one organisation to another? Can the organisations trust the training staff theologically? Will they, in the end, be willing to employ our trainees? How will sending organisations be represented in the decision-making processes of the programme? How committed will they be to helping the programme? Are there parts of the training task they will be asked to look after? If the training is for a single agency or denomination, will the training fit into the overall strategy of the organisation?

In what country is the training programme located?

Are there legal or economic limitations on how the programme can function? Are there cultural expectations about how a training programme operates or the awards that should be given to those who complete it? If so, do these expectations conflict with attitudes the programme wants to inculcate? What should be done about this conflict?

Who is available to staff the training programme?

What individuals are qualified to serve as administrators and teachers? Are any of these people available to work with the programme full time? If not, what are their schedules? Could they help part time? Who is available but not yet qualified? What could be done to train these potential staff members?

Staff selection is the single most important factor in the effectiveness of any missionary training programme. If the staff themselves are experienced missionaries whose lives are marked by personal holiness and a zeal for world evangelisation, these qualities will be communicated to trainees as well. Experience teaches us, however, that any staff member who lacks these qualities or who is oriented toward scholarly recognition or toward personal power and esteem, despite many other positive qualifications, will diminish the effectiveness of missionary training and may become an instrument to turn the programme away from its original training objectives.

What outside partners or sponsors will have
an interest in the programme?

Should foreign donors and staff be used for the programme? If so, who are they and how can they be contacted and interested? What are their expectations? Are there strings attached to their help which need to be considered? Does the programme need to conform to some standards set elsewhere?

The potential for foreign funding is understandably attractive to many who consider starting new missionary training programmes, but it can be a dangerous snare. From many parts of the world we receive reports about training programmes which lose the support of their national church when they are perceived as funded from abroad. In other cases, leaders of training programmes who look abroad for financial support seem to develop an independence from their national Christian brothers and sisters which is both unattractive and unhealthy. Whenever funding for a training programme comes from the churches it exists to serve, on the other hand, natural accountability structures exist. In addition, the missionary involvement of the national church is developed through its participation in the missionary training programme.

Making the Administrative Plans

We previously noted that starting a missionary training programme cannot and must not be the personal project of a single individual. Nevertheless, such a project needs at least one person with vision, drive, and commitment to see the dream come true. Unless someone expresses this vision, shares it with others, and rallies others who are prepared to explore missionary training opportunities and needs, nothing will happen.

So many people need to cooperate for a missionary training programme to succeed that unless they all "own" the project, progress will be hindered. Key people whose cooperation is needed must take part in making decisions about the programme very early on. We have referred to this group as a training committee.

Once it is clear that a missionary training programme is needed and once the type of people who are likely to use the programme is defined, decisions must be made. It is wise at this point to assemble a working group. This group may consist of the training committee plus church leaders and representatives of the missionary sending organisations to be served. Having a number of people involved in decision making brings wider expertise to the plans.

As the project continues and administrative policies are drawn up, however, a board can be formally constituted. All those who ought to have a say in how the programme is run should be represented on the board, including all cooperating sending organisations. The board sets policies and oversees the work of the training programme. It usually makes sure that the money is handled properly and that the policies it approves are carried out. It meets from time to time to hear and deliberate on reports by those delegated to carry out decisions. These delegates eventually include the administrative staff.

As soon as the board is formed, some kind of constitution or set of regulations for conducting the business of the programme should be drawn up to clarify the authority structure. Under the board, some programmes have a person who oversees the daily work, such as a principal. Other programmes are run by a committee of leaders or rotate leadership among the staff.

The way authority is handled and the structures for handling it will affect the atmosphere and learning experience in the programme. If we want to inculcate a servant spirit among the missionaries we are producing, the leaders of the programme need to model a servant leadership style. These things are part of the informal curriculum discussed elsewhere in this manual.

The board plans how to accumulate the spiritual, human, physical, and financial resources needed for the missionary training programme. It makes decisions about how to get staff and students. It also looks for finances and other physical resources. It promotes the programme with publicity and raises up prayer support. Three important questions which need to be considered by the board relate to setting admission standards for admitting trainees, procuring and handling funds, and raising public aware-ness and prayer support.

Selection of Trainees

If the training is for missionary candidates, the sending organ-isations should do the grass-roots recruiting, while the programme staff should encourage and assist the sending organisations to supply trainees. A programme aimed at pre-candidates can recruit trainees directly. In either case, not everybody proposed for the training may be able to benefit from our programme, and we may not have room to take everyone who applies. We need some criteria to know whom we should train.

Trainee selection policies should reflect the purpose of the training programme. If the training programme is aimed at pre-candidates, the selection criteria may not be too stringent. Pro-grammes for missionary candidates need clearly stated selection criteria.

There is little debate that missionary candidates must be committed Christians who feel called to missionary service. They need to be emotionally mature and otherwise personally suitable. It is difficult to find out these things just from a single personal interview. Recommendations from the church and from other spiritual mentors of the candidate need to be obtained. Pro-grammes that take only trainees sent by a missionary sending organisation allow the organisation to screen the candidates. Even then, clearly stated admission policies will help the sending organ-isation staff determine when candidates are most likely to benefit from the training our programme provides.

In-service training programmes for people who are experienced missionaries should require recommendation from the missionary sending organisation. While admission qualifications may not be so important, clearly stated programme purposes and objectives are essential.

Some training programmes insist that married candidates must both qualify as students and come as a couple. This is less common for non-residential training programmes or short semi-nars. We need to pay attention to training couples, however, since they will work as a team on the mission field. Both the husband

and the wife need to understand what missionary life and ministry are all about.

Is there any question about the applicant's proficiency in the language in which training is conducted? If so, we need to test for that. Do we expect applicants already to have a certain level of Bible knowledge? Then we need some evidence of their attainment in this area.

Are we running a programme for trainees who have attained a certain educational level? People of varied educational backgrounds can be mixed profitably in informal and nonformal learning situations, but this is more difficult in formal settings. If a certain academic attainment level is expected before admission to our programme, how does this affect the recognition and perceived qualification of our graduates? How does it affect teaching styles?

Funding and Accounting

Few training programmes feel they have no worries about funding. Most missionary trainers rely on the Lord and need to pray for the resources to run their programmes. Often the programmes that do the best in this regard are those sponsored by an established denomination or by an independent mission agency with a reasonable support base. Even a denominational training centre can face problems, however, if the churches of the denomination have not caught the missionary vision. Often one of the tasks of a missionary training programme is to spread mission awareness and vision among its constituency. People do not give to programmes or projects which do not catch their interest and zeal. The programme as a whole, from the board to the trainees, needs to make funding a constant matter of prayer.

Programmes run jointly by several missionary sending organisations experience more problems. Unless all the partners are committed to owning and providing for the programme, everybody's business tends to become nobody's business. Sending organisations may wonder if they would not be better able to bond trainees to their home and field staff if they did all the training themselves. They find it difficult to squeeze from their meager resources money and manpower to support a programme that is not fully their own. They may feel that other partners are not putting in their own share, so why should they? They may find that the programme is not meeting their organisational needs adequately and so hold back from fuller involvement. This may lead to a situation where the programme staff must win greater commitment from partner organisations, must restructure the programme, or must close the missionary training centre.

Joint programmes, however, can make good sense in stewardship of resources, since together, sending organisations can afford what individually they cannot. Trainees gain by exposure to other organisations, and the pool of trainers is larger. If a joint effort is being considered, it is important to get very firm commitment from the partners before beginning. This requires whole-hearted agreement about the aims and policies of the programme.

Training programmes of small, less established organisations seem to suffer the most financially. Sometimes missionary training does not have the glamour of missionary work to attract donors. The programme may be unrecognised by any government or official body, so trainees are unwilling to pay large fees. These programmes need to align themselves with specific missionary sending organisations or join some kind of fellowship which can bring them to the attention of donors and provide input for their improvement.

There are two main sources of funding for missionary training programmes:

- fees paid by trainees or by the organisations sponsoring them
- donations from the Christian community, including both local and foreign donations

Fees need to be set to meet as much of the expenses of running the programme as the trainees can reasonably be expected to pay, given their financial background. In a few cases this could be 100%, but this is rare even in affluent countries. Awareness and publicity also are needed to attract local donations. Encourage visits to your programme or to your graduates in their fields. Take presentations to churches and fellowships.

Foreign donors usually are most interested in giving for one-time capital expenses (like buying equipment and facilities) rather than recurrent expenses (like salaries and office supplies). They also usually want a lot of reports, pictures, etc. They may specify how the donated money may be spent. Sometimes these restrictions are due to government regulations about charitable giving in their own country. Whether you appreciate their attitude or not, if you want these donations you must respect the conditions under which they are given. Many recipients from the Two-Thirds World resent what is perceived as a paternalistic attitude on the part of Western donors. Whenever you accept large amounts from anyone, however, the factor of donor control comes into play, no matter who the donor may be. If you don't like this situation, avoid these donations. In any case, only accept donations for projects that are in line with your own priorities.

As noted above, large donations from abroad also can make local donors lax about supporting the missionary training programme. There may be quarrels about how the money should be spent. Staff and students may have raised expectations about what they are entitled to, financially. For these reasons, experience indicates that cultivation of local donations is safer and wiser. If foreign donations are accepted, the more people who are involved in planning how outside aid will be used, the better. The whole situation needs to be bathed in prayer.

Sometimes staff can be funded by personal support-raising, just as many missionaries do. At other times staff may be seconded and paid by a cooperating organisation. They model dependence on the Lord for their own support to the students, who will have to do the same. It is important, however, that sponsors of a training programme should not purposely under-support the staff. Whenever this occurs, the sponsors are communicating something about their attitude toward the worth of missionary training work!

Some missionary training programmes have had success in adding to their income by practical projects done by the students, such as a dairy project which sells milk or an agricultural project which helps feed the students.

Proper arrangements need to be made for keeping the accounts of the programme. If the accounts can be audited regularly, this will increase the confidence of people who want to give and will provide a good example to the trainees of financial honesty and accountability.

Publicity and Prayer Support

A missionary training programme needs prayer support as much as missionaries on the field. So much of what needs to be accomplished in the lives of trainees has to be done, in the final analysis, by the Holy Spirit. We cannot neglect doing something, therefore, to generate intercession on our behalf. Most programmes have a newsletter or a column in a mission publication to make known information about the programme. This also may be an avenue to raise finances and recruit students. Specific prayer points should be given for the programme, along with news of answers to prayer.

Besides using printed publicity, missionary training programmes should train students to present the work of missions and missionary training, and they should provide opportunities for students to do so in churches and fellowships. In addition, a programme that goes out of its way to serve missionary sending organisations in promoting missions will be noticed and appreciated. This means we should be ready to help others with their own training programmes, especially with literature and visiting teachers.

A training programme also can organise prayer seminars and can encourage the setting up of support groups who pray for and help with the programme.

Starting a Missionary Training Programme in an Established Theological Institution

An established institution has traditions of administration, curriculum, and ethos which can seldom be changed overnight. If missions has never been a noticeable part of the programme, any effort to introduce missions must overcome considerable institutional inertia.

The first step often is to convince those who shape the curriculum that mission studies are important. These people should be the targets of mission awareness efforts through personal conversation, presentations, survey trips, student requests, encouragement from larger movements such as the AD 2000 Movement, and missions literature. If the institution's leadership is ready to promote missionary training, a lot can be accomplished in a short time.

If support for missionary training is weak, however, those trying to get missions into the theological school may have to be content to work gradually. The contagiousness of their own passionate commitment to world evangelisation and their on-going involvement in missionary outreach, local and remote, may be their most powerful strategy. At the same time, however, they can work toward the introduction of core missions courses, one by one, into the existing curriculum. They can identify courses already being taught which would be part of a missions curriculum (such as World Religions or Church Planting), and they can pass on resources to the teachers of these courses to give more missiological content. As time goes on and demand increases, they can ask for a missions minor and finally a missions major to be offered in the school. Some schools are used to the idea of departments, and a missions department can be proposed. In other schools, departments are not used, so it may be harder to know the status of the missions courses. This may be an opportunity to infuse missions into the entire curriculum, rather than isolate it in a department.

The people interested in teaching missions also need to keep looking for materials giving a missiological perspective, that they can pass on to teachers in other departments, such as Bible, theology, or Christian education.

Barbara Burns lists the advantages and disadvantages of missionary training in a theological school in her article "Missionary Training Centres and Theological Education Institutions" in *Internationalising Missionary Training*. Students in theological schools are exposed to a broader range of Christian studies as a context for the study of missions. They also can develop more in-depth Bible knowledge, and they have time to digest what they are learning. The school benefits as well by having mission insights added to balance other disciplines. The Great Commission stands at the heart of the Christian faith and, strange as it may seem, schools which separate biblical and theological studies from missions are irresistibly drawn toward a scholastic orthodoxy and an impotent faith. It may take time before teachers desire and understand how to integrate the mission insights into other disciplines, but when they catch the vision for missions they will become our great allies in preparing good missionaries.

Some theological schools are better than others at the kind of lifestyle training that comes from the informal educational experiences of school life. Usually as the push for a large enrollment increases (often for economic reasons), the harder it is to maintain the community life and devotional atmosphere of the school. It may be that only the missions teachers consciously model a missionary zeal and lifestyle; if so, some missions students may be carried away by other ambitions. When the student-to-teacher ratio is high, missions teachers also have less impact per individual student. The length of a school's programme also gives time for missionary zeal to ebb.

Some schools do internship and field work well, and this emphasis can provide an opportunity for mission internships. Other schools concentrate on classroom work, so major adjustments need to be made for missions students. Since missions internships often entail travel, which costs money, special fundraising efforts may be needed to cover these expenses.

Once a theological school has established a missions department or major, our focus can shift to developing a missionary training programme using steps similar to those listed previously.

Conclusion

We need more missionaries in the world today if we are to finish obeying Jesus' last command. This probably means that we need more missionary training programmes. One of our most serious limitations, however, is the availability of qualified trainers. We must not be discouraged by this shortage, because training that is less than ideal is better than no training at all. When Jesus told us to pray labourers into the field, surely he also meant labourers who would train the others. As we face the challenge in missionary training around the world, let us commit ourselves to prayer that God will see his programme accomplished in the earth.

Chapter 8

Fighting the Enemy with New Methods

Rodolfo Girón

1 Samuel 17 records the account of David and Goliath. It also tells the way Saul responded to David's brave offer to fight the giant. This historical text relates one of the most significant moments in the life of the people of Israel. It is a model passage, demonstrating the importance of using appropriate and contextualised methods to fight the enemies we face as the people of God.

This application is particularly true for the missionary movement from the Two-Thirds World, as it relates to traditional missions from the West. Methods, tools, and strategies that may have been of great value to the development of the historical movement may not fit the needs and potentials of emerging Two-Thirds World missions. In the area of training, this recognition is especially valuable. We may have a tendency to adopt the methods of others uncritically, because we feel they have worked well for some cultures. At the same time, some may attempt to impose their methods on us, just because they believe theirs is the right way to do missionary training.

In its own battlefields, the non-Western missionary movement is facing a lot of giants like David's Goliath. This man was physically greater than David. He was almost three metres (9 feet, 9 inches) tall, and David was but a "young man" by comparison. Goliath was there to fight the trembling flock of Israel. No one, not even big King Saul, was ready to fight him.

David came as someone simply willing and able to fight the great giant. David proved to be a man of vision, courage, and valour, but beyond this, a man filled with the Spirit of God. The way David faced the battle using his own methods, his own experience and tools, is an example to us as we try to approach the challenge of developing training methods and strategies to train our missionaries who are going to face the big giants on the mission field. We can simply repeat what others traditionally have done, because such an approach is believed to have worked well, or we can identify and use our own methods that fit our realities and needs.

Let's see how David faced the different challenges before him.

The Challenge of Confronting Opposition and Criticism

One of the major problems we can face when we offer to fight giants is the opposition and criticism that comes from our own people. It doesn't make sense, but we can be defeated even before entering the battlefield. This is exactly what David faced when he decided to ask, "What will be done for the man who kills this Philistine and takes away the reproach from Israel? For who is this uncircumcised Philistine, that he should taunt the armies of the living God?" (v 26, NASB).

First, David encountered opposition from his brothers (vv 28-29). According to verse 28, when Eliab, his older brother, heard of David's interest in what was happening, he spoke to him saying, "Why have you come down? I know your insolence and the wickedness of your heart...." Instead of being proud of David's valour, David's brother was angry with him. Unusual as it may seem, David did not stop to argue but "turned away from him." The point is not to turn away from our own people, but we should turn away from the "loser mentality" that refuses to believe that we are able to do great things with God's help. Following David's example, Two-Thirds World Christians in any nation need to embrace a "winner mentality." The time has come to believe that we are able to do things far beyond our own limitations. We need a change of mentality.

The second kind of opposition David faced came from the establishment—from King Saul (vv 33-37). David's offer finally came to Saul's attention. It is remarkable to see David's courage in saying to the King, "Let no man's heart fail on account of him [referring to Goliath]; your servant will go and fight with this Philistine."

Saul's response to this brave declaration clearly indicated his prejudice due to David's appearance. He said to David, "You are not able to go against this Philistine to fight with him, for you are but a youth while he has been a warrior from his youth."

It is easy to discount somebody because of his or her appearance or apparent inexperience. Saul failed to consider David's own resources and experience. According to the text, he did not even remember who David was (see v 55). Some time ago I read a commentary on this passage by a Latin American theologian. He observed that because David's name and record were not in Saul's computer, this did not necessarily mean David did not exist. Like David, the Two-Thirds World missionary movement can be dismissed as "not able" and "too young" to fight the giants of Islam, Hinduism, and other false religious systems.

David's response to Saul's prejudice was not a self-defence or an apology, but it was a reaffirmation of his own principles and experience. David's mind was clear. He did not take time to address Saul's prejudice and fears. Instead, he directly told Saul about his past experiences. "Your servant was tending his father's sheep. When a lion or a bear came and took a lamb from the flock, I went out after him and attacked him and rescued it from his mouth.... Your servant has killed both the lion and the bear, and this uncircumcised Philistine will be like one of them since he has taunted the armies of the living God."

David understood God's power in his life. He knew he was able to defeat Goliath because God was with him. When we know for sure what we are able to do through the power of the Spirit of God, we do not need to apologise for what God has done through us.

Here we need to consider the importance of the recent history of Christianity. In the last three decades Christianity has experienced a paradigm shift. While in the past most Christians were in the West, now the great majority are in the non-Western world. The church is growing fastest in countries such as Korea, China, Guatemala, and Brazil. The fact is, many things are different now from before. Churches in many countries have come of age; they have learned their own ways of doing things. God has blessed Two-Thirds World churches in such a way that many churches in the West have begun to learn from them.

The Challenge of Choosing the Right Methods

Like most people, Saul believed it was impossible to fight without proper armour. Therefore, he did what he considered proper; he determined to clothe David with his own armour so David would be able to face the giant. He never thought to ask whether his armour would fit David. He did not consider if, instead of helping David, his armour would hinder him. Saul just thought, since his armour worked for him, it will work for David. Does that sound familiar? It frequently happens when we try to solve problems in other cultural contexts. We assume our own methods must be the best for the people we are working with.

Here is a case in which someone with experience on one battlefield tried to impose methods on another person who was new to this kind of fighting, although he had fought his own battles. It is worth noting that David did not refuse to try the armour. He gave it a chance, but he soon found out that it was not the best way for him to enter the battle. Many times, we try methods other than those we are used to. It is good to try, especially when we are in a pre-field situation. Nevertheless, we will find that some methods and strategies will not fit our needs or resources.

We see what happened with David; verse 39 says, "And David girded [Saul's] sword over his armour and tried to walk, for he had not tested them." Lack of practice with Saul's armour left David unable to use it. In spite of the convenience of advanced methods used by others, if we are not familiar with them, they may not work for us.

Realising that he could not use Saul's methods (his armour and sword), David "put them off." He then took up his own weapons and used his own strategy to fight. David "chose for himself five smooth stones from the brook, and put them in the shepherd's bag ... and his sling was in his hand and he approached the Philistine" (v 40). David knew what he was able to do with the things that were familiar to him.

What a tremendous message from this passage to the Two-Thirds World missionary movement! We need to remind ourselves that during the past fifty years, we have learned many good things. The church in the Two-Thirds World is growing faster than ever and much faster than in the West. The largest churches are in the Two-Thirds World. Many wonderful things have been accomplished in what was called the "mission field." Now is the time to use those experiences to enter the battlefield against such giants as Islam, Buddhism, and Hinduism.

There is no better tool than the one we know how to use well. This does not rule out the possibility of being trained in the use of new tools, but even the way training is done should be adapted to the mentality and need of those receiving the training. The question arises, How can those from other contexts pass on valuable experiences without imposing methods that do not fit the needs of the new fighter? How can we apply training experiences and methods that have proven effective in Western countries, but which may not be the best for our particular situation? I will say the answer is contextualisation.

We have to learn how to take advantage of tools and methods used in other contexts, taking the core principles and applying them to our own situation. In a sense, David did this when he defeated Goliath. Verse 51 says, "Then David ran and stood over the Philistine and took his sword and drew it out of its sheath and killed him and cut off his head with it." David used Goliath's sword to finish his task, but he did not depend on it. We need to learn how to take the best things from others and apply them to our need in a contextualised way.

David is a great example to us. While he was experienced and had faith in what he knew God could do through him, he did not refuse to give Saul's methods a try. Nevertheless, he was courageous enough to say, "I cannot go with this. Saul, I cannot do it your way; let me do it my way. God has shown me different methods for fighting the battle, and I trust they will work with this giant." David's goal was to give God the glory and honour. He was not looking for his own exaltation but for God's. When answering Goliath's challenge he said, "I come to you in the name of the Lord of Hosts, the God of the armies of Israel, whom you have defied.... This day the Lord will deliver you into my hands ... that all the earth may know that there is a God in Israel" (vv 45-46 RSV).

David's ultimate goal was that all the earth would give glory to God—the only one who deserves it!

This is a great example to us; the glory in all we do belongs to God. Sometimes when we do things in a different way, we do not receive recognition. Others may gain credit, but that does not matter since we are seeking God's glory. We are looking at the ultimate goal—that all the earth, all the people on earth, all those unreached with the gospel—may know that there is one God who loves them and sent his Son Jesus Christ to die for them.

What a lesson for us! A youngster, led by the Spirit of God to fight the enemy in an unconventional way, teaches God's people that it is possible to win the battle using methods that fit our realities and resources, and in doing so to give all the glory to God.

Appendix A

Biblical-Educational Commitments to Guide Missionary Training

1. Training objectives should be determined by the understandings, skills, and qualities required for effective service.

2. Training is "church related"; learning occurs best in the context of community.

3. Training structures and relationships must be consistent with training goals.

4. Training strategies should be appropriate to the learner's ways of thinking and learning.

5. Training strategies should incorporate and build upon the learner's experience.

6. Theory should be validated by Scripture and by general revelation.

7. Information should be appropriated and obeyed.

8. Skills-learning should include instruction, demonstration, and guided practice.

9. Character qualities and values are effectively communicated only when teaching includes modelling and reflection.

10. Training equips the learner for effective ministry and continuing growth.

Appendix B

Missionaries' Competencies Profile: Argentina[1]

First Southern Cone Consultation of Mission Trainers
July 18-20, 1991, Córdoba, Argentina

In the following profile, training areas are listed in **bold** type, with competencies listed under each training area.

Church Relations

- Is a committed member of a church
- Maintains a good testimony
- Knows how to subject self to church authorities
- Knows how to inform the church on the missionary task
- Understands the vision of the church
- Has the support of the church to go as a missionary
- Exercises an approved ministry in the church
- Knows how to maintain communications with the church
- Knows how to relate to other church bodies

---

1. Due to the small page size of this book, it has been impossible to reproduce this chart in its original form. The original chart was published, however, in *Training for Cross-Cultural Ministry*, vol 91, no 2 (September 1991), pp 4-5, and in *International Journal of Frontier Missions*, vol 10, no 2 (April 1993), p 84.

Cultural Anthropology

- Is able to analyse his own culture
- Is conscious of his own ethno-centricity
- Is informed on ethnic groups within the country
- Respects other cultures
- Knows biblical anthropology
- Can contextualise biblical principles
- Creates a kingdom culture
- Has short-term missionary experience
- Can see with anthropologist eyes
- Can adapt to another culture

Interpersonal Relationships

- Applies biblical principles to relationships
- Knows how to manage interpersonal conflicts
- Maintains good family relationships
- Looks for relationships with others unlike self
- Maintains a good attitude when criticised
- Has a basic understanding of psychology
- Knows how to listen to others and respond appropriately
- Has experience in community-based living
- Knows how to relate on intimate terms

Cross-Cultural Communication

- Knows the host culture
- Is willing to identify with host culture
- Knows what communication is
- Knows how to manage culture shock
- Values all without racial prejudice
- Is willing to incarnate self
- Confronts communications problems
- Interprets verbal and nonverbal messages
- Distinguishes biblical principles and customs
- Can detect cross-cultural bridges for evangelism

Linguistic Orientation

- Is disciplined and persistent
- Knows language acquisition techniques
- Is willing to learn
- Is humble and uninhibited
- Can laugh at own errors
- Knows the rules of phonetics
- Can recognize idiomatic gestures and terms
- Has experience with language learning

Biblical Knowledge

- Is convinced that the Bible is the Word of God
- Knows and loves the Bible
- Knows how to conduct exegesis and interpretation
- Knows geography, customs, history, canon, etc.
- Understands that the Bible contains the solution to human problems
- Knows how to teach the Bible using various methods
- Applies biblical message to own daily life
- Knows the biblical basis of mission
- Has the habit of memorising scriptures
- Knows inductive Bible study methods

Theological Knowledge

- Knows God, his person, and his work
- Understands God's mission
- Knows the doctrine and plan of salvation
- Knows the function and mission of the church
- Knows the concept and scope of the kingdom
- Knows church growth principles
- Knows systematic theology
- Knows contemporary theological currents
- Has knowledge of different religions
- Knows how to defend the authenticity of the Bible

Leadership

- Is sensitive to the voice of God
- Knows how to work with a team
- Knows how to delegate responsibility
- Plans and establishes objectives
- Encourages, motivates, and transmits vision
- Knows own limitations
- Has experience as a leader
- Knows how to detect and use others' gifting
- Serves with renouncement
- Shows flexibility

Discipleship

- Has been discipled
- Shows sensitivity to the newly converted person
- Is a model disciple and is worthy of being imitated
- Transmits life as well as knowledge
- Has knowledge of pastoral counselling and inner healing
- Shows love for own disciples
- Knows strategies and methods for discipleship
- Is a mentor
- Forms disciples who in turn disciple others

Evangelism

- Evidences a strong spiritual life
- Knows the message
- Demonstrates a passion for souls
- Knows how to communicate adequately
- Practises personal evangelism
- Knows how to prepare evangelistic sermons
- Knows methods and techniques of evangelism
- Knows how to identify with the person with whom sharing
- Knows how to respond to problems and objections

Emotional Health

- Has been approved for the field emotionally and psychologically
- Has resolved significant emotional problems
- Is open to receiving counsel for emotional health
- Demonstrates an adequate self-image
- Maintains emotional equilibrium
- Is constant in motivation towards what he begins
- Knows how to manage failure
- Is approved physically to live on the field
- Practises a hobby, pastime, or sport
- Takes weekly and annual breaks

Spiritual Life

- Is building an intimate relationship with God
- Knows the power of prayer and fasting
- Knows the principles of spiritual warfare
- Studies the Bible systematically
- Demonstrates the fruit of the Spirit
- Uses his spiritual gifts
- Shows an attitude of service
- Demonstrates moral integrity

Christian Ethics

- Knows biblical ethical principles
- Analyses cultural norms in terms of biblical principles
- Shows courage in conducting himself according to his values
- Can facilitate the adoption of an indigenous biblical ethic
- Is honest, just, and upright
- Respects established laws and regulations
- Knows the difference between ethics and doctrine

Practical Abilities

- Knows how to take advantage of the situation
- Knows how to "grow, raise, and repair"
- Knows how to apply community help
- Has working skills
- Has knowledge of crafts and recreation
- Knows how to perform household duties
- Knows how to operate electronic equipment
- Has knowledge of first aid medicine and hygiene
- Has knowledge of preventive medicine
- Has musical knowledge

Appendix C

Qualifications for Indian Missionaries[1]

The following list of qualifications for Indian missionaries was compiled by participants in a consultation and workshop called by the Indian Missions Association and jointly sponsored by the Missions Commission of the World Evangelical Fellowship. The consultation was held September 21-23, 1992, in Madras, Tamilnadu, India.

Attention in the workshop focused on identifying "character qualities" and "ministry skills," with the understanding that informational requirements should be instrumental to character and ministry ends. The workshop format did not afford opportunity to classify or prioritise character qualities and ministry skills.

CHARACTER AREAS

1. Spiritually Mature

The missionary is...
- Spiritually and morally discerning
- Characterised by "the fruit of the Spirit"
- Growing in Christ-likeness
- Lovingly committed to reading the Bible
- Prayerful

---

1. Originally published in *Training for Cross-Cultural Ministry*, vol 92, no 3 (November 1992), pp 4-5.

- Committed to (and actively exercises) spiritual disciplines
- Committed to (and actively participates in) a local church
- Biblically oriented (applies biblical values to things, people, and relationships)
- Cooperative
- Sensitive to the needs of others

2. Zeal for Cross-Cultural Evangelism

The missionary is...

- Burdened for the unreached millions
- Faithful in evangelism (i.e., shares the gospel with non-Christian neighbours)
- Eager to learn about evangelistic needs (evidenced by reading missionary biographies and gathering information about evangelistic needs)
- Committed to pray urgently and specifically for world evangelisation
- A motivator of others to pray for missions
- A liberal financial supporter of world evangelism
- Committed to obediently respond to God-given vision
- Committed to accept an on-going life of suffering
- Joyfully accepting of difficult conditions, without self-pity
- Committed to follow Christ's model of passion and brokenness
- Committed to practise a simple lifestyle

3. Disciplined and Accountable

The missionary is...

- A careful steward of time, money, spiritual gifts, and personal health
- In control of one's speech
- Faithful in keeping one's word
- Committed to (and practises) a lifestyle of mutual submission
- Acknowledging of and submissive to authority
- Committed to exercise authority appropriately

 • Clean and wholesome in one's personal habits

4. Adaptable

The missionary is...
 • Willing to adapt in one's role and vocation
 • A humble learner
 • Positive and hopeful despite adversity
 • Patient and uncomplaining
 • Focused on one's purpose
 • Appreciative of the good in another culture

5. Rightly Related to God

The missionary is...
 • Reverently submissive to God
 • Prayerfully adoring of God
 • Experientially aware of the power and authority of Jesus
 • Confident of God's faithfulness
 • Conscious of God's presence

6. Rightly Related to One's Family

The missionary is...
 • Committed to reserving quality time for constructive relations with one's spouse and children
 • A spiritual leader in one's home
 • Committed to demonstrate and cultivate openness, sharing, submissiveness, and love
 • Encouraging in relationships with one's family members
 • Positive regarding one's own self-image

7. Rightly Related to One's Community

The missionary is...
 • Respected by one's neighbours (maintains good rapport)
 • Appreciative of the positive side of people
 • Helpful (looks for opportunities to serve one's neighbours)
 • Empathetic (shares the joys and pains of one's neighbours)

MINISTRY AREAS

1. Exercises Spiritual Disciplines

The missionary is able to...
- Pray persistently and effectively
- Praise God appropriately and give him the thanks he is due
- Faithfully intercede for others
- Practise waiting on God
- Study the Bible for personal and ministry enrichment
- Meditate on God's Word
- Lead in family prayers
- Develop and use a prayer calendar
- Fast

2. Engages in Spiritual Warfare

The missionary is able to...
- Apply Jesus' power in one's personal life
- Apply Jesus' power in cases of spiritual bondage
- Engage in spiritual battle whenever required
- Resist the devil by faith, prayer, and fasting
- Discern the spirits

3. Communicates Effectively (in one's own language)

The missionary is able to...
- Carry on intelligible, interesting, and helpful conversations
- Speak effectively in public gatherings
- Write interesting and effective letters and reports
- Keep a personal journal

4. Builds Relationships and Friendships

The missionary is able to...
- Understand different personalities
- Accept people as they are
- Listen attentively and perceptively

- Maintain awareness of one's own perspective
- Discern the boundaries of appropriate communication
- Positively contribute to others
- Appreciate and encourage others
- Manage conflict
- Forgive and ask forgiveness
- Delegate responsibility

5. Understands and Communicates Cross-Culturally

The missionary is able to...

- Expose and reject ethno-centrism (is a bridge builder)
- Adopt local culture where appropriate (incarnational model)
- Learn the local language and thought patterns
- Learn nonverbal signal systems and cultural forms
- Learn cultural roles and relationships
- Identify with the people
- Understand decision making structures and hierarchies

6. Learns a Language

The missionary is able to...

- Recognise the imperative of language learning
- Build friendships
- Observe and listen perceptively to language sounds and patterns
- Imitate local speakers
- Patiently persevere in language learning
- Regularly practise speaking the language

7. Evangelises and Preaches

The missionary is able to...

- Build positive relationships which express Christian love
- Discern the readiness of non-Christians to hear the gospel
- Express Christian truth, exposing spiritual error
- Apply the Bible to bring conviction of sin

- Express the gospel clearly and effectively
- Use a variety of methods (including indigenous) to share the gospel

8. Teaches, Trains, and Disciples

The missionary is able to...
- Lead a personal or group Bible study
- Make truth simple, interesting, and attractive
- Communicate clearly, with sensitivity to one's listeners
- Plan for and encourage discipleship and servant leadership
- Set an example in prayer, Bible study, personal discipline, and character

9. Plants the Church

The missionary is able to...
- Survey the field
- Set specific goals and targets
- Evangelise by appropriate means (witness, Bible translation, literature distribution, house visitation, personal counselling, etc.)
- Teach and train new believers for discipleship, stewardship, and worship
- Organise believers into a self-governing, self-nurturing, and mission-oriented congregation
- Equip believers to indigenise the church
- Train believers for E-1 evangelism

10. Manages Time and Resources

The missionary is able to...
- Use a diary, day-planner, year-planner to plan ministry involvement and personal time
- Be conscious of time, but with flexibility
- Use waiting time profitably (redeem one's time)
- Balance priorities of time and relationships
- Recognise and develop one's own and others' gifts

- Keep accurate financial accounts

11. Copes with Stress and Loneliness

The missionary is able to...
- Understand one's own limitations
- Understand cultural and environmental limitations
- Understand one's expectations of self and others
- Pace oneself, taking time for rest and restoration
- Apply God's standard to one's work load
- Maintain awareness that others face stress and limitations
- Build one or more relationships of accountability and sharing
- Accept help from others

Appendix D

Profile of Asian Missionary Trainers: Philippines[1]

Titus Loong/Stephen Hoke, Manila, June 10, 1993
(EFA Missions Commission)

Spiritual Maturity

- Evidences a winsome, growing, close walk with God; consistent prayer life; prays regularly with spouse; fasts
- Studies Bible daily; honours the Word of God in his daily life and manifests fruits of the Holy Spirit
- Aware of the principles of spiritual warfare and willing to handle biblically
- Knows and uses his spiritual gifts while not abusing them
- God-fearing; sensitive to God's will and guidance; demonstrates moral integrity
- Evangelical in doctrine

Missionary Experience

- Has demonstrated effectiveness in cross-cultural ministry, preferably for some years (with team experience)

---

1. Due to the small page size of this book, it has been impossible to reproduce this chart in its original form. The original chart was published, however, in *Training for Cross-Cultural Ministry*, vol 93, no 2 (August 1993), p 6, and in *Mission Frontiers Bulletin*, vol 16, no 1-2 (January-February 1994), p 50.

- Has fruitfully planted a growing and mission-minded church or has solid experience in a range of church-based mission activities
- Has positively contributed to the national church and has been an effective team member in church or missions
- Effective in communicating the gospel
- Recommended by both his church and mission board; accepted by fellow missionaries and national leaders
- Brings to the training community a specific contribution from his particular mission ministry

Academic Qualifications

- Training should demonstrate a diversity of knowledge, learning, and abilities
- Some may have formal degrees (Bible, theology, missions, linguistics, administration); others are graduates of missionary training programmes
- Still others train and minister out of their total life experience in missions; the issue is effectiveness as missionary trainers
- Field experience is required; academic qualifications (M.Div., M.A., or M.Th. in Missions) or the equivalent is preferable
- Committed to biblical/evangelical missiology; able to discern and correct non-biblical influences in ministry

Teaching Skills

- Effective communicator/motivator for missions
- Effective teacher
- Stays current in missiological issues/trends and strategic developments
- Always growing in use of educational tools
- Welcomes dialogic education; able to facilitate interactive learning
- Sensitive to differences in teaching and learning styles

Family Life (if married)

- Maintains healthy family life; communicates well with spouse and children
- No major unresolved conflict within the family
- Husband and wife can work as a team
- Family members are physically fit and emotionally healthy
- Maintains a balance between family life and ministry responsibilities
- Willing to use home for hospitality and fellowship

Christian Ethics

- Practises principles of biblical/Christian ethics
- Can distinguish what is culturally and biblically acceptable from what is not
- Observes and respects local laws and customs in light of Christian ethics
- Contextualises without syncretising

Church Relations

- Is an active member (or pastor) of a local church, contributing with his/her gifts
- Is committed to church-based missions outreach
- Has solid experience in a range of church-based ministries; willing to submit to spiritual authorities
- Recommended by local church (and denomination when appropriate)
- Can communicate missions in the local church
- Has a high view of the church in the target country and can coach and mentor emerging church leaders

Interpersonal Relationships

- Positively affirms others; not monopolising or domineering
- Willing to listen, especially when corrected
- Relates properly to opposite gender, locals, superior, employees; not over-intimate nor cold

- Experienced in community living; can manage conflict without explosion or hiding emotions
- Relates well with people of different personalities and cultural backgrounds
- Good verbal and nonverbal skills; friendly, not overly dependent; knows how people feel about him/her

Cross-Cultural Awareness and Skills

- Has broad cross-cultural experience; understands cross-cultural principles
- A continuing learner of cultures; can see with "anthropological eyes"; approaches cultures without prejudice and with perceptiveness
- Quick to adapt to new culture situations; able to identify with the people
- Respects and affirms all ethnic backgrounds
- Can discern whether to accept customs or not; finds functional substitutes
- Has won acceptance and respect of host culture; has experience in ministry to Asian religions and cultures

Leadership Skills

- Has a positive track record of follower-ship and servant-hood
- Apt to be a role model
- Has a positive track record of leading/influencing others by character, credibility, and competence
- Willing to listen to new ideas and able to discern priorities; plans ahead yet flexible when necessary
- Committed and able to recruit and train new trainers; seeks to bring out the best in trainees
- Exhibits good management and administrative skills; willing to delegate; not controlling

Discipleship Skills

- Has been discipled; has been a good example to fellow missionaries

- Advises and counsels with trainees' temperaments in mind
- Experienced in pastoral counselling; vulnerable
- Models loving openness and acceptance in mentoring
- Committed to value of upward, peer, and downward mentoring
- Has gifts of a mentor/trainer/equipper/encourager

Self-Esteem and Emotional Health

- Emotionally stable; healthy and healed from past hurts; has a positive self-image
- Has a joyful, confident view of life and ministry; able to handle stress
- Able to forgive and resolve problems
- Understands place of pastoral care and counselling for missionary nurture; has basic listening and counselling skills
- Admits failure and shows evidence of growth and change
- Manages leisure time and finances well; no undesirable habits

Integrity and Accountability

- An honest and upright person
- Responsible to finish tasks with good results and on time
- Does not make vague promises; does not over-expect from others or self
- Not lazy nor underestimates self
- Demonstrates good stewardship of private and public money
- Responsible to report to and be accountable to sponsoring church or agency

Attitude to Asian Missions in Global Perspective

- Zealous toward Great Commission and Asian context and contribution
- Affirms and develops the identity of Asian missions; can adapt patterns and principles to Asian context

- Learns from the history/experience of missionary movements of other regions, but not subservient to them
- Has a growing understanding and appreciation for holistic ministry among the poor
- Committed to train Asian missionaries; works well with Western or non-Western personnel
- Enters into cooperative and strategic partnerships between Western and non-Western missions

Appendix E

Essential Attributes of a Missionary Trainer[1]

Missionary Training Consultants' Seminar
February 22-26, 1994, Pasadena, California

This report summarises the work of the Two-Thirds World regional working groups at the WEF/MC-sponsored Missionary Training Seminar in Pasadena, California, February 22-26, 1994. This document is a composite profile of attributes of a missionary trainer's life and ministry that are key essentials leading to a successful training ministry. The majority of the groups identified each of these attributes, although the wording greatly varied among the groups.

Christian Maturity

- Maintains spiritual disciplines in personal relationship with God
- Is building an ample knowledge of the Word of God
- Is growing in obedience to God's Word
- Is characterised by the fruit of the Spirit
- Practises an effective prayer life
- Promotes a biblical relationship with the church
- Exercises good stewardship

---

1. Due to the small page size of this book, it has been impossible to reproduce this chart in its original form. The original chart was published, however, in *Training for Cross-Cultural Ministry*, vol 94, no 1 (April 1994).

- Gives priority to a balanced family life
- Lives a sacrificial and simple lifestyle
- Has vision and a passion for mission
- Builds accountability relationships
- Is respectful of spiritual authority
- Possesses a teachable spirit

Ministry Skills and Experience

- Has successful cross-cultural experience in ministry
- Develops effective disciple and mentor relationships
- Is able to manage people and projects with sensitivity and wisdom
- Interacts well with others in cross-cultural and diverse situations
- Has personal maturity to sustain open and honest relationships
- Enters into cooperative relationships with diverse peoples
- Demonstrates cultural sensitivity and respect

Teaching and Equipping Skills

- Is a good listener and effective communicator
- Focuses on practical and relevant course work
- Is able to teach using various techniques and resources
- Brings a wealth of practical and personal experience
- Can foster good interpersonal and team dynamics
- Accurately evaluates people and guides them to effectiveness
- Models by lifestyle what is being taught
- Motivates people to want to learn

Interdisciplinary Knowledge

- Relates theological knowledge to missiological practice, especially regarding socio-political, economic, and ethical realities
- Is familiar with local, political, and social situations and organisations

- Has prior training and experience appropriate to the institution's goals
- Keeps abreast of other missionaries and mission activities worldwide
- Has a biblical and historical grasp of the local and global church

Appendix F

Principles of Curriculum Planning

Three basic principles—continuity, sequence, and integration—will help you in the process of planning your curriculum and organising learning experiences (Tyler 1949:84-86).

Continuity

Continuity refers to the repetition or recurring emphasis of major curriculum elements. The trainer seeks to achieve a flow or connection between different units of learning so that there is an unbroken unity and cohesion to what is being learned.

- A young convert may receive teaching on communion and later receive further Bible institute or seminary instruction on the same subject.
- Principles for culture learning that are acquired pre-field should be reinforced by on-field internship and mentoring by experienced missionaries.

Trainers must recognise the necessity of providing recurring and continuing opportunities for these skills to be practised.

Sequence

Sequence stresses organising instruction over time (i.e., longitudinally) in a way that encourages meaningful learning. Each successive experience should build on the preceding one, with increasing breadth and depth.

- Succeeding exercises in preparing a sermon should stretch trainees into broader issues and push them deeper into disciplined biblical study. Merely repeating an assignment at the same level leads to little or no positive development in attitude, understanding, or skill.
- Development of observation and culture learning skills should focus on more complex social situations, broader hypothesis formation regarding behaviour, and greater depth of analysis.

In this way, a second-year missionary would not simply repeat the learning experiences of the first year, but would explore the surrounding culture more broadly and with more depth of insight.

Integration

Integration refers to organising concurrent instruction so that topics and principles in various subject areas "fit together." The organisation of learning experiences should help trainees gain a holistic perspective by discovering ways in which all the separate pieces fit together into a cohesive whole.

Integration of learning activities involves pointing out patterns and relationships (e.g., between church history and missions strategy, between culture and evangelistic methods). Integration is the process of drawing linkages between evangelism and discipleship, between "pastoring" and "teaching" skills, between one's personal character (being) and ministry effectiveness (doing).

Appendix G

LESSON PLANNING SHEET

UNIT TITLE: _____

UNIT GOAL: _____

_____

Lesson Title: _____

Focal Passage: _____

Background Passage: _____

Lesson Goal: _____

_____

Lesson Objectives: *To achieve this goal the learner will...*

1. _____

_____

_____

2. _____

_____

_____

3. _____

_____

_____

Materials Needed:

-
-
-
-
-

Lesson Outline:

Notes:

Appendix H

Sample Course Evaluation Questionnaire

Course Title: Ministry Training for Church Leadership
Instructor: Robert Ferris

COURSE EVALUATION

I am committed to being the best teacher I can be and to making my courses as valuable as possible for my students. Since I am scheduled to teach this course again next year, I need your help. I WOULD APPRECIATE YOUR MARGINAL COMMENTS AND SUGGESTIONS ELABORATING OR SUPPLEMENTING THE ITEMS ON THIS QUESTIONNAIRE. I assure you, I will read them all.

The course objectives are listed below. Please indicate the level to which you feel we realised these objectives.

Objectives	TR	SR	NR
	TR = Thoroughly Realised		
	SR = Somewhat Realised		
	NR = Not Realised		

1. Be able to summarise the biblical role of leadership in the church as a worshipping, nurturing, evangelising, and redemptive community. ___ ___ ___

2. Be able to summarise how the traditional approach to ministry training developed. ___ ___ ___

<u>**Objectives**</u>	**TR**	**SR**	**NR**
3. Be able to summarise how theological education by extension (TEE) developed.	___	___	___
4. Be able to explain the implications of biblical doctrine for ministry training.	___	___	___
5. Be able to explain the implications of adult education principles for ministry training.	___	___	___
6. Be able to evaluate traditional and TEE approaches to ministry training according to biblical and adult education principles.	___	___	___
7. Be able to list innovations in ministry training and evaluate their strengths and weaknesses according to biblical and adult education principles.	___	___	___
8. Be able to apply biblical principles and recent innovations to develop appropriate new programmes of ministry training or to renew existing ministry training programmes.	___	___	___

QUESTIONS ABOUT COURSE PROCEDURES

9. I required you to read a book of your choice on leadership and write a four-page review. Was this a useful assignment?

   ___ Yes, do it again.

   ___ Keep the four-page review, but assign the book to be read.

   ___ No, omit this assignment.

10. I selected readings for discussion each day of class. On the whole, did you find these readings helpful?

   ___ Yes   ___ No

Was the class time spent discussing these articles well invested?

____ Yes

____ I would prefer more time allocated to:
        ____ Lecture
        ____ Discussion of biblical passages
        ____ Small group work/presentations
        ____ Other: _____

11. I required you to submit a reading report. Did I provide leads to enough books and articles?

    ____ Yes   ____ No

Did the titles on my bibliography address your interests and concerns?

    ____ Yes   ____ No, I would like more guidance to:

    _____

Did you use the notebooks of collected readings which I placed on library reserve?

    ____ Yes   ____ No

12. I required you to participate in a group which prepared a paper and class presentation on one aspect of leadership. Was this a useful assignment?

    ____ Yes, do it again.

    ____ It was okay, but one or two persons inevitably get stuck with an unfair amount of the work.

    ____ I appreciate your intent, but our group found it difficult to work together.

13. When I required you to work in a group, I intended to encourage helping and sharing (vs. competition) among class members. Was this a useful method? (Check all appropriate responses.)

    ____ Yes, do it again.

    ____ This really did not affect the "culture of competition" in the class.

14. I asked you to grade the members of your group. My purpose was to afford due recognition to those who contributed most to the group's project (which I could not observe). Was this a fair procedure? (Check all appropriate responses.)

    ____ Yes, do it again.
    ____ I really don't think student-assigned grades are fair.

15. I intended to model in and out of class an approach to ministry training which is consistent with the principles discussed in this class. What comments or advice do you have that can help me improve in this area?

16. What other comments or suggestions would you like to pass along about this course? (Use the back of this sheet, as necessary.)

It is not necessary to sign this evaluation form; I will value your comments whether you do or do not.

Appendix I

A Brief Review of Programme Evaluation in America

Educational programme evaluation emerged in the United States as a discipline field in the 1960s. At that time, the federal government began investing heavily in national and local education programmes, with an accompanying demand for accountability. Early evaluation theory advocated a "goals based" approach, assessing programme outcomes in terms of stated goals. In 1972, Scriven published a critique of goals-based evaluation in which he decried the particularity of this approach. By focusing evaluation exclusively on a programme's stated goals, Scriven argued, the evaluator is guilty of a kind of "tunnel vision," ignoring unanticipated outcomes which may be significant, both positively and negatively. As a corrective, Scriven called for "goal-free evaluation." While Scriven's proposal was not taken seriously, his critique of goals-based evaluation was; programme evaluators were sensitised to the importance of unanticipated outcomes.

The next major development in evaluation theory came in the early 1980s. To that point, evaluation had focused on the educational process. Stake (1983) identified two approaches to evaluation—the "institutional self-study by staff approach" and the "student gain by testing approach." Although these approaches varied sharply in the formality of research methods employed, neither looked beyond the educational process and its immediate outcomes. Through the 1970s, however, educators became aware of the centrality of values in the educational process and of the larger social context of education. As evaluators struggled with these realities, the concept of "stakeholders" developed, with a recognition of the importance of factoring stakeholders' expectations and needs into the evaluation process. Thus, "responsive evaluation" was conceived in response to these recognitions.

Currently, emphasis within the accreditation community in the United States has shifted to "outcomes research." To the extent that new seriousness has been directed toward the products of education versus the processes, this is a positive move. The struggle continues between "goal based" evaluation and "responsive evaluation," with its sensitivity to the role of values and social context. In practice, "goal based" procedures still predominate. Leading programme evaluators, however, continue to call for more informed approaches to educational assessment. After reviewing alternative perspectives on evaluation, Bogue and Saunders conclude:

> [These commentaries] remind us first that no organization—corporate or collegiate—can ignore its environment and expect to have success in responding to and shaping its future. Any sensible vision of quality, then, must involve sensitivity to some of these environmental forces. Second, strategy embraces those assumptions and values that guide our approach to the future (Bogue and Saunders 1992:258).

It is comments like these which underline the strategic importance of responsive evaluation and which give hope for the future.

Reference List

Benson, Warren S. 1993. "Setting and Achieving Objectives for Adult Learning." In *The Christian Educator's Handbook on Adult Education*, ed. K. O. Gangel and J. C. Wilhoit, pp 162-175. Wheaton, IL: Victor Books/SP Publications.

Bloom, B. S., ed. 1956. *Taxonomy of Educational Objectives. Handbook I: Cognitive Domain.* New York: McKay.

Bogue, E. G., and R. L. Saunders. 1992. *The Evidence for Quality.* San Francisco: Jossey-Bass Publishers.

Bolton, N. 1977. *Concept Formation.* Oxford: Pergamon Press.

Botterweck, G. J. 1986. "*yada'.*" In *Theological Dictionary of the Old Testament*, ed. G. J. Botterweck and H. Ringgren, pp 448-481. Grand Rapids: William B. Eerdmans Publishing Company.

Brookfield, S. D. 1986. *Understanding and Facilitating Adult Learning.* San Francisco: Jossey-Bass Publishers.

Dettoni, John. 1975. "Writing Spirit-Led Objectives," pp 4-9. From Leighton Ford's Reachout Series. Minneapolis: Billy Graham Evangelistic Association.

———. 1993. "Introduction to the Teaching Ministry of the Church." Course syllabus. San Clemente, CA: Chrysalis Ministries.

Eisner, Elliot W. 1969. "Instructional and Expressive Objectives: Their Formation and Use in Curriculum." In *Instructional Objectives: An Analysis of Emerging Issues*, ed. W. J. Popham, pp 13-18. Chicago: Rand McNally.

Elliston, Edgar J., ed. 1989. *Christian Relief and Development: Developing Workers for Effective Ministry.* Dallas: Word Publishing.

Elmer, D. 1993. *Cross-Cultural Conflict: Building Relationships for Effective Ministry.* Downers Grove, IL: InterVarsity Press.

Ferris, R. W. 1989. "Accreditation and TEE." In *Excellence and Renewal: Goals for the Accreditation of Theological Education,* ed. R. L. Youngblood, pp 59-79. Exeter, UK: Paternoster Press.

———. 1990. *Renewal in Theological Education: Strategies for Change.* Wheaton, IL: Billy Graham Center.

———. 1992. "A Four-Step Process for Curriculum Development." *Training for Cross-Cultural Ministries,* vol 92, no 3 (November), pp 6-7.

Ferris, R. W., D. Esterline, J. Gullison, R. K. Hart, and G. D. Samuel. 1986. "Accrediting TEE: Steps Toward Understanding and Practice." *Theological News/Theological Education Today,* vol 18, no 4 (Oct-Dec), pp TET 1-10.

Fisher, R., and W. Ury. 1991. *Getting to Yes: Negotiating Agreement Without Giving In.* 2nd ed. New York: Penguin Books.

Gagné, R. M. 1985. *The Conditions of Learning.* 4th ed. New York: Holt, Rinehart and Winston.

Galvin, J. C., and D. R. Veerman. 1993. "Curriculum for Adult Education." In *The Christian Educator's Handbook on Adult Education,* ed. K. O. Gangel and J. C. Wilhoit, pp 178-189. Wheaton, IL: Victor Books/SP Publications.

Gangel, Kenneth O., and James C. Wilhoit, eds. 1993. *The Christian Educator's Handbook on Adult Education.* Wheaton, IL: Victor Books/SP Publications.

Goad, Tom W. 1982. *Delivering Effective Training.* San Diego: University Associates.

Groom, Thomas H. 1980. *Christian Religious Education.* New York: Harper and Row.

Guba, E. G., and Y. S. Lincoln. 1983. "Epistemological and Methodological Bases of Naturalistic Inquiry." In *Evaluation Models: Viewpoints on Educational and Human Services Evaluation*, ed. G. F. Madaus, M. Scriven, and D. L. Stufflebeam, pp 311-333. Boston: Kluwer-Nijhoff Publishing.

Harley, C. David. 1995. *Preparing to Serve: Training for Cross-Cultural Mission.* Pasadena, CA: William Carey Library.

Huebner, Dwayne. 1975. "The Tasks of the Curricular Specialist." In *Curriculum Theorizing*, ed. William Pinar, pp 250-270. Berkeley, CA: McCutchan Publishing Corporation.

Joyce, Bruce R. 1978. *Selecting Learning Experiences: Linking Theory and Practice.* Washington, DC: Association for Supervision and Curriculum Development.

Kemp, Jerrold E. 1977. *Instructional Design: A Plan for Unit and Course Development.* Belmont, CA: David S. Lake Publishers.

Knowles, M. S. 1980. *The Modern Practice of Adult Education.* Rev. ed. Chicago: Follett Publishing Company.

LeBar, Lois E., and James E. Plueddemann. 1989. *Education That Is Christian.* Wheaton, IL: Victor Books.

LeFever, Marlene D. 1990. *Creative Teaching Methods: Be an Effective Trainer.* Elgin, IL: David C. Cook Publishing.

Mager, Robert F. 1975. *Preparing Instructional Objectives.* 2nd ed. Belmont, CA: Fearon Publishers.

Massey, Brian. 1994. Personal letter to William D. Taylor, August 8.

McKean, Rodney. 1977. Unpublished notes, College of Education Doctoral Seminar. East Lansing, MI: Michigan State University.

Mitchell, B. J. 1983. *DACUM.* 4 vols. Richmond, BC: Ministry of Education.

Moon, S. C. 1994. "Who Are the Korean Missionaries?" *The Pabalma.* An occasional paper of Korea Research Institute for Missions, Seoul, Korea.

Norton, R. E. 1985. *DACUM Handbook.* Columbus, OH: Ohio State University, Center for Research in Vocational Education. (ERIC: ED 254 657)

Pasmino, Robert W. 1987. "Curriculum Foundations." *Christian Education Journal*, vol 8, no 1 (Autumn), pp 31-44.

Pate, L. D. 1991. "The Dynamic Growth of Two-Thirds World Missions." In *Internationalising Missionary Training*, ed. W. D. Taylor. Exeter, UK: Paternoster Press.

Plueddemann, James E. 1987. "Curriculum Improvement Through Evaluation." *Christian Education Journal*, vol 8, no 1 (Autumn), pp 55-60.

———. 1991. "Purposeful Stumbling About in Search of Surprises." *Bridge: Wheaton Graduate School Alumni Newsletter*, Fall.

———. 1994. "Behavioral Objectives, No! Faith Goals, Yes!" *Intercom*, no 144 (August-October), p 8.

Plueddemann, James E., and Carol Plueddemann. 1990. *Pilgrims in Progress: Growing Through Groups*. Wheaton, IL: Harold Shaw Publishers.

Schon, Donald A. 1983. *The Reflective Practitioner*. New York: Basic Books Inc.

Scriven, M. 1972. "Pros and Cons About Goal-Free Education." *Evaluation Comments*, vol 3, no 4 (December), pp 1-4.

Sinnett, W. E. 1976. *The Application of DACUM in Retraining and Post-Secondary Curriculum Development*. Toronto, ON: Humber College of Applied Arts and Technology. (ERIC: ED 119 013)

Stake, R. E. 1983. "Program Evaluation, Particularly Responsive Evaluation." In *Evaluation Models: Viewpoints on Educational and Human Services Evaluation*, ed. G. F. Madaus, M. Scriven, and D. L. Stufflebeam, pp 287-310. Boston: Kluwer-Nijhoff Publishing.

Swamidoss, A. W. 1994. Personal letter to R. W. Ferris, December 28.

Taylor, W. D., ed. 1991. *Internationalising Missionary Training*. Exeter, UK: Paternoster Press.

Tyler, Ralph W. 1949. *Basic Principles of Curriculum and Instruction*. Chicago: University of Chicago Press.

Unger, M. F., and W. White, Jr., eds. 1980. "To know." In *Nelson's Expository Dictionary of the Old Testament.* Nashville: Thomas Nelson Publishers.

Ward, Ted. 1975. Unpublished notes, College of Education Doctoral Seminar. East Lansing, MI: Michigan State University.

————. 1979. Unpublished notes, College of Education Doctoral Seminar. East Lansing, MI: Michigan State University.

————. 1982. "Nonformal Education—What Is It?" In *Nonformal Education: Reflections on the First Decade,* comp. T. Ward, L. Joesting, and L. D. Horton, pp 8-12. East Lansing, MI: College of Education, Michigan State University.

————. 1994. Personal conversation with S. Hoke, July 18.

Windsor, R. V. J. 1995. *World Directory of Missionary Training Programs.* Pasadena, CA: William Carey Library.

Index